Snack Yourself Slim

Richard J. Warburg, PhD, JD
Tessa Lorant, MA

The Thorn Press

The advice, information and guidelines given in this book are not in any way intended to replace professional medical advice. Any reader, particularly one with a preexisting medical condition, should consult with a doctor before starting on this program.

All reasonable care has been taken in preparing this book; neither the authors nor the publisher can accept responsibility for any consequences arising from the use of this information.

ISBN: 978-0-906374-05-4

The Thorn Press
Lansdowne House, Castle Lane, Southampton SO14 2BU, UK
www.thethornpress.com

Printed in the UK and the US

CONTENTS

INTRODUCTION

The eminent and respected biochemist, Dr. Kenneth Buechler, summarizes the **EATALL™ WAY** as follows:

This is a sure-fire way to lose weight and still enjoy eating.

It's not a question of whether this **EATALL™** non-diet plan, or constant snacking, will work for you. It *will* work, and you *will* lose pounds, inches and – even more importantly – fat. The only issue is whether you can fit the new regime into your daily life for a few days, preferably a few weeks. After that it becomes habit and you'll find it easy. The snacking has been tested by scientific experiment and by many individuals. Not only do you lose fat but you gain a healthier body by reducing cholesterol, and hence the risk of heart disease.

The other pertinent question is how healthy can you be *while you snack*. Can you be good and avoid sugar-rich foods and unhealthy meats? Or will you resort to the less healthy (but equally effective from a weight loss point of view) use of poor dietary foods? Will you increase the speed of success by exercise, or will you remain a couch potato? So the question with this non-diet *snacking* is not can you get it to work for you, but just where can you cut corners and 'cheat' so that you remain on the non diet and are happy. That's what this book is about: we show you how you can enhance your ability to succeed, how to increase the opportunity for you to adapt to a new way of life, and how to see the lean self hidden inside what now exists.

There's another bonus: this non diet works in such a way that you can lose those tough last few pounds you always promised yourself you would lose. But, importantly, it also helps to reduce those too-large dimensions around the waist and thighs. So read the book. Do the best you can. 'Cheat' as needed and benefit from this proven way to obtain your new 'hot bod'.

PROLOGUE

Richard's Discovery

I came up with a way to lose weight that my friends tell me they already know. Of course, none of them are actually using the method, or know how to apply it. But they all seem to think they know about it when I tell them. That is clearly a good sign – everyone already knows it will work! Not only that: but when you go back to the literature you see tons of support – no pun intended. Everyone agrees that eating more frequent meals is a good way to control weight – then, for some mysterious reason, these same people keep encouraging you *not* to snack.

Indeed, it turns out the method was used tens of thousands of years ago – long before people started to eat meals on a regular basis. Our ancestors were hunter/gatherers who ate as they roamed their area. Hunting and gathering – foraging – was the way all human beings lived until around eight thousand years ago, when agriculture was invented. We've progressed way beyond that – we forage in supermarkets and fast-food outlets for instant meals including hot dogs and hamburgers. And we're expecting our bodies to cope with this enormous change in a relatively short time. Not all are able to.

Back around April 2006 I'd been trying to get down to 168 lb from around 172 lb. Well, OK, so maybe it was 173 lb or 174 lb, but don't push it. It seemed simple to lose just six pounds, and I did. The problem was that I could never maintain that lower weight. That doesn't sound all that meaningful for people trying to lose a substantial amount of weight, I know. Actually, it's very significant. The hardest part of losing weight is taking off those last ten pounds or so. A method which works for that will readily work for taking off any amount of weight.

Like everybody else, I've seen all those programs, and read all those books, telling me to exercise, to eat special foods, even to go on a diet! I tried a few of them, but as soon as I ate the next meal my weight went back up. Exercise didn't work for me either; nor did one meal a day, a regime I was perfectly comfortable with.

I keep pretty busy so not having meals was just fine by me, and I gulped one down in the evenings, thinking that might work. I was fed up with all those companies trying to sell me special foods, fancy machines to work out on, whatever – they were just trying to take my money.

However, I had seen this one advertisement about the body going into fat storage mode when it's being starved, and explaining that metabolism increases with five rather than three meals a day. This piece of information appealed to me; it fitted in with my scientific background in a way all those other ads and fads did not – it made real sense. That's when it occurred to me that one really should eat all the time.

That idea, and being too cheap to try the diet meals being sold, started me off. I simply acquired all the foods I enjoy eating: apples, tomatoes, a few grapes, a handful of nuts, crackers, wafers, chocolate-covered pretzels, even chocolate itself… I simply started eating anything small and easily portable. And I just ate one or two of these snacks every thirty to sixty minutes. Around meal times I ate maybe a little extra – more as a treat than anything else. The key point was that I didn't eat meals; I substituted eating snacks at frequent intervals instead.

I never got hungry, and my body 'reset' within two days. I found I'd lost weight – about 2 lb if I could trust my scale. Which, in fact, I didn't really, but it made me feel good.

I continued with my new plan, but I didn't weigh myself regularly. What's more I worked out less than usual simply because I was too busy in the office.

I weighed myself again after a week and found I was down to 163 lbs. I assumed my scale was wrong so I went to the fancy one at the gym. They barely recognized me since I hadn't been there in so long. Anyway, I'd always felt that if you pay for gym membership you shouldn't actually have to work out as well. I weighed myself on their machine. That one has to be accurate, right?

I *had* lost weight! I was at 163 lbs – I should have trusted my own scale in the first place. It was a wonderful feeling – I'd lost all the weight I'd wanted to lose, and more, without even trying.

I was very comfortable with the new eating regime. Now I was just munching on fruit, vegetables, hors d'oeuvres at parties, whatever. Well, OK I did eat a lot of chocolate too – but that is a staple I can't do without. The key was a lot of small 'meals' – I didn't know what else to call them then. Basically, I could eat whatever I liked, just never eating too much at any one time. At meal times I had a couple of extra pieces of whatever I enjoy, then kept right on eating that way for the rest of the day.

Very soon I couldn't even stand the idea of a whole meal. A single bagel seems huge to me now. Within only two weeks my pants were falling down. Even my abs were getting into shape – or simply visible.

That's when I decided to do some research on what was going on. It seemed a good idea to ask others to try the system out, and to see if this way of eating was easy to maintain. What I specifically wanted to know was: was the **EATALL™** way really a new way to eat? And was it also a way to be healthy? It turns out it's both, and I have been eating this way ever since.

My co-author, as well as several friends and acquaintances, have also been using the **EATALL™** way successfully. Together we will share our experiences, and our suggestions on how to make this method work for you.

A BRIEF OUTLINE OF THE EATALL™ WAY

Here we spell out the bare bones of the **EATALL™** way. If you have no time or inclination to read anything else in this book this will get you started on a new way to eat – and enjoy – your food.

The EATALL™ way to eat is to consume one EATALL™ portion at each EATALL™ time. The size of the portion and the timing may vary, but there should generally be just enough food to keep hunger away during each 45-60 minute period. The overall food for the day needs to be chosen so that all necessary nutrients are eaten each day.

Please note: we aren't trying to sell you anything. We're not selling food or equipment. The **EATALL™** way is *free*. We know that it can be commercialized, and if it catches on so be it. That will just make those of us who are too busy or lazy to focus on such matters more likely to comply. So here is the method in a nutshell, based on an average person's food needs for a single day. The method will need tweaking for smaller or larger people as detailed later in this book.

After the first couple of days you can 'cheat' and not feel guilty. Once you've 'reset' your body it takes more than a single cheating moment to unset it. Try to avoid cheating in the first two days, but don't stop the **EATALL™** way simply because of it – *it will still work*. After the first couple of days you can cheat more often without much guilt at all – that means you can fail to eat for a few hours, or have a huge meal, and still get right on with the **EATALL™** way again and not be punished too much by your body putting on pounds.

Here are the seven most relevant points to remember

1. Eat as soon as you get up, until an hour or so before you go to bed.

2. Eat at least every hour, and eat enough so you don't feel hungry. We call these EATALL™ times.

3. Don't eat more each day than you used to eat each day.

4. Pick any foods you like to eat, but eat only a small portion at a time.

5. Keep the food out of sight so that you're not tempted to eat more, or more frequently.

6. Drink constantly if possible, but try to avoid drinks with sugar or caffeine,

7. If you like to exercise that is always good.

Those are the six easy steps to follow. We've fleshed them out a little for you below:

Once you're up, eat at least every hour, and eat enough so you don't feel hungry. We call these **EATALL™** times. When you start eating the **EATALL™** way, just eat a little something every fifteen to thirty minutes for the first two hours. Or start immediately after a meal. That way you'll get rid of any hunger issues.

Pick any foods you like to eat, but eat only a small portion at a time: a small bunch of grapes, a few crackers, a small bowl of mashed potato, between one and four slices of lean meat, a small to medium apple – you get the idea. Try to ensure that the total amount of food eaten in any one day is the same as or less than what you used to eat. If you like to count Calories, try to keep the total Calories in any day to that recommended for your size, weight and activity levels.

It's expedient to keep food out of sight so that you're not tempted to eat more, or more frequently. The idea is to keep a steady stream of food in your stomach. You'll find your stomach will feel fuller as time progresses; it will 'shrink' so that when you look at 'normal' food portions you'll wonder how you ever ate them all at one sitting.

Preferably choose foods low in sugar and fat. Try to choose some with high fiber. The easy choices are whole grain crackers, low-sugar dried or regular fruit, nuts, cheese, sliced meats, regular foods you eat at meals, anything that you enjoy so you'll have variety, nutrition, and not get bored.

It's useful to drink constantly, if possible, because it will make you feel full. Try to avoid drinks with sugar, and with caffeine, if you can. Don't sweat it if you simply cannot do that; just try to cut down on them as much as possible. Water is always good. Note that a drink counts as eating if it contains Calories – a can of cola or a glass of milk or even a glass or wine or beer, for example.

Though this method is in no way a Calorie counting method, it is useful to recognize the **EATALL™** portions you will use for your own particular method of eating the **EATALL™ way.** Generally, you can eat anywhere around 100 Calories of any food – you can find snacks in precisely those quantities all over the grocery stores these days. The choices are tremendous – you can just buy whatever you enjoy eating in ready-to-go-packs and the rest of the method will be easy.

If you prefer to make up your own portions, one site among many on the web provides a great list for you to choose from:

www.goodhealth.com/articles/2007/08/20/100_calorie_snacks

Put 'Calorie' into Google and find many more such sites. Please bear in mind that sites change quite frequently, so be sure to search for the latest ones.

We call these amounts **EATALL™** portions. Several ways of putting them together are suggested in the chapter on **IDEAL EATALL™ PORTIONS** near the end of this book.

> *We'd like to stress one very important point: do not eat more than you need to keep hunger at bay.*

You should see some weight loss in a couple of days – maybe just a pound or two, but in a week there should be a significant loss. Don't get too hooked on your scale, weight can fluctuate for all kinds of reasons: an inaccurate scale, standing the wrong way, different clothes, water retention or simply the time of day and proximity to any exercise. A better guide is to notice how your clothes feel on you. Looser is good.

The first two days are the most critical so try to focus on those for a really good chance of success. Don't expect too much, relax. Just get used to this new way of eating your food for the day.

When choosing a large fruit, like a banana for example, just eat a part of it, and keep the rest for later. You can even freeze it so it doesn't go off – or you can just put it in the refrigerator to eat later that day. Share your food with a companion non-dieter.

Get used to doing what your mother told you not to do – leave lots of food on your plate and waste it. The starving children in India won't benefit if you eat it all – how could they? If you really want to help starving people send the money you'll save by putting less on your plate to begin with. You'll learn in due course how to ensure you put the right amount on your plate in the first place.

Remember that if you join other people for meals, especially for eating out, and more particularly when you or someone else is paying big time for the privilege: keep on track by eating slowly and by chewing each mouthful until it is small enough and dissolved enough to be swallowed easily. Alternatively, cheat that one time. The **EATALL**™ way is meant to be relaxing, not prohibitive.

Take one or two hours for that kind of meal, give yourself time to savor it, enjoy talking to your fellow diners. After all, it's a fancy occasion and someone is paying for it.

One good strategy is to order appetizers only – you may actually prefer the taste, you can always have more than one, and the choice is often much more varied and unusual than the entrées. As long as you're not simply focusing on the food but talking, or even listening, to your fellow diners, say, you'll be fine. You can also work out your own ideas to make this way of eating easier for yourself page:

Here are three suggestions for putting the **EATALL**™ way into effect when eating in a restaurant:

1. Have the salad dressing put on the side so you have to 'play' with the food a little. It's possible to take over an hour to eat half a salad, and then leave the rest as you'll feel full.

2. Use chopsticks whenever possible. If you don't know how, that's even better: it will slow you down. When you do know how to use them you'll realize they're fantastic for picking up tiny scraps of food at a time. A forkful, by contrast, may pick up far too much.

3. Don't order all the food at once. Start with one appetizer.

Since you're not hungry, this last suggestion should be easy. Order that first appetizer, then eat it – slowly, of course. If you're still hungry after you've finished, or are still having a good time and want to prolong the meal, order another appetizer. Maybe even decide to splash out on an entrée.

You can, after all, leave most of it and ask the restaurant to bag it. Then use the leftovers as one **EATALL™** portion or more for the next day.

You'll work out many more methods for dealing with eating out for yourself.

THE EATALL™ WAY IS NOT A DIET

R eally, hand on heart, it isn't. **No diet – NO diet – NO DIET!**
The **EATALL™** way is a method of waist and weight control so simple that it can be summed up in one sentence:

> *Forget meals; instead, consume EATALL™ portions throughout your waking day at frequent, approximately hourly, intervals.*

That's it. You'll have a hundred questions as to what, and how, and why, and we'll try to address all of those. But, basically, all you have to do is to reeducate yourself to eat small amounts throughout your day – and get used to forgetting about meals.

This is going to require a rethink of the way you organize your life, depending on whether you live alone (easiest), with a partner, what your work circumstances are, how you interact with your family – it will even depend on your health. What we can promise you is that there *is* a way to have this method work for everyone, and a relatively easy one at that.

The **EATALL™** way is nothing more than making a number of adjustments – not even major ones when you look into it. The problems that do arise are, partly, matters of habit but, more importantly, pressures – peer pressures – from the society we live in.

Our lives tend to center around meals: breakfast, lunch and dinner. Many of us already skip breakfast – which is the worst thing you can do from a weight control point of view, especially if you use the diet approach. We also use meals as social and business occasions. That's set in our collective unconscious, and has been, for generations. These considerations turn out to be the biggest problem when applying the method, not the method itself. That can easily become your norm within two to three weeks, which is the time it takes to change a habit. Eating fixed meals at fixed times is simply a habit, nothing more.

Let's just go back to the diet mentality which, in the developed countries, is also part of our collective experience since the turn of the twentieth century. Before that food was scarce and expensive, and large numbers of people worried more about whether they would get enough to eat rather than the effect that eating too much might have on their bodies. It wasn't until relatively recently that food became cheap enough, and plentiful enough, for the majority of people living in the affluent parts of the world to have sufficient to eat.

That sufficiency has become plenty. Plenty which, in a way, made people slaves to cooking. Three square meals a day take hours to prepare.

In due time cooking gave way to going out, then to 'take out' (which actually means bringing it in), TV dinners from the supermarket and, finally, instant food – and instant gratification. That's what triggered the phenomenal success of the companies which provide instant food and, it would seem, instant weight gain.

So there's the problem: we have cheap, plentiful, tasty food in every store carrying food, and in restaurants and takeouts on every street corner in every town. You don't even have to sit down to eat. You can buy a hot dog, eat it as you walk or drive, or buy a hamburger and take it away in a box complete with fries and the sugar rich ketchup it always comes with, plus toys for the kids. There's pizza and taco, noodles, fish and chips, Indian and Thai, Mexican and Chinese, bagels and doughnuts. The choice is exotic, the service quick, the price affordable.

The price in health is not so cheap: you only have to look around you to see expanding waistlines, wobbly bodies oozing over airline seats, oversize clothing stores multiplying fast. Restaurants have been forced to increase their chair sizes. And the cost in health – well, lack of health – is dramatic. Diabetes is rampant, with seniors aged sixty-five and over having a much too significant chance of contracting it. That disease is linked to being overweight. Heart disease is also increasing. It has become the number one killer and is linked to overindulgence in the wrong kinds of fat.

To counter this explosion another one has taken place. Diets galore, taking up the best-seller slots on the non-fiction lists, advising eating plans and exercise routines. And there are many diets to choose from – literally a thousand or more. As each new diet book is published it's bought by increasing numbers of frustrated dieters – they've tried the one which came out last month, and that didn't work. Now they'll try the new one in case it does the trick for them.

The fact is that, in all likelihood, each one of those diets has something to contribute – if only you can stick to it. It may not be entirely healthy, or a permanent answer, but it will have the germ of help with weight control.

Some simply ask that you eat less food at meal times – well, that seems pretty obvious. None, however, seem to address the issue of the food that is all around us, and how to be able to eat that food without gaining weight.

But, if you scan through most of these diets, and then look through the hundreds of diet books that have been spawned, you'll notice that there's one interesting fact missing. Many of them agree that eating more meals is a good idea. Some even suggest three meals and three snacks every day. The point they make is that you ensure that you're hungry when you eat. They suggest that it's a bad thing to eat when you're not hungry.

That's where the **EATALL™** way differs radically. The problem with allowing yourself to get hungry is that food, once again, dominates your thoughts. What *is* being hungry? Do you use the first little nudge, which might just be because you see someone else eat, or smell some attractive food? The supermarkets know all about that one. The smell – not always the actuality – of freshly baked bread gets those juices going, as does the smell of freshly brewed coffee. They actually manufacture the smell to tempt you.

By the time you feel real hunger it's too late for rational eating, just as waiting to be thirsty before drinking is already the sign of dehydration.

Many popular diets claim that some people eat when they're not hungry simply because it's time for a particular meal, or for some other social reason. Even a study suggesting having seventeen meals in one day still discussed meals.

That is perhaps the biggest problem. Diets are based around meals. Taking time to have meals is so engrained that we cannot stand to miss them, or do without them.

Meals aren't, of course, the only problems with diets. In some cases they ignore food altogether: they suggest you stop eating, for example. Not a helpful or healthy solution. Other diets are pretty complex. You're required to weigh the food, calculate the number of Calories, in fact turn eating into a major arithmetical undertaking. First buy a calculator...

That's when we realized that the best inventions are the simplest. Yes, we can always make dieting look complex, but the principle stays the same – not to eat more than the body requires for your lifestyle. KISS – Keep It Simple Stupid.

This is where we say it again – just eat so that you don't get hungry by using regular **EATALL™** portions. That way you'll never eat too much. This method works with all the known diets (except perhaps the starvation ones) even if they tell you not to snack – just ignore them, otherwise do what they suggest. Do check with your doctor if you have special health requirements and make sure you get his or her approval.

Let's review a few of the better-known diets over the next few pages. All have been highly lauded at some time. Several continue to be used around the world. They work, but they do have some drawbacks. However, most can be combined with the **EATALL™** way to make them work better and to be very much easier to follow.

The Starvation Diet

We all know the simple way of losing weight – don't eat at all. But, broadly, it's hardly the preferred method. There are a number of well-documented downsides – you'll probably lose muscle as well as fat, and you'll feel terrible. A common problem found using a starvation diet is that, once the dieter returns to normal eating, weight is regained – rapidly. Worse, the regained weight may be fat rather than muscle so that the chance of maintaining the newly gained weight is increased.

And, amazingly, starving yourself is not the quickest method of losing weight. The body notices the lack of food, panics, and slows its metabolism. You can live a long time without eating, weeks rather than days. But, do remember, you can only live a short time without water.

The Catabolic Diet

Dr Victor Lindlahr came up with a diet which prescribed certain foods as taking up more Calories via digestion than were actually eaten. He didn't mention the amount of the food, but the diet went with a six hundred Calorie restriction for the day. It's an interesting concept. What is also true is that many of his so-called 'catabolic' foods are high-fiber, high-bulk foods which help to keep you feeling satisfied while eating fewer Calories.

A more recent version of this is **The Negative Calorie Diet**. We all realize that any food has some Calories. However, certain low Calorie foods in relatively small amounts actually do require more Calories to digest than the food itself provides. This will lead to the body using up stored fat and can be taken as a basis for a diet.

The so-called negative Calorie foods are, for the most part, the bulky vegetable foods such as salad leaves, broccoli and cabbage, cucumbers and celery. Even the most determined vegetarian would have trouble living on just those foods, and we all know the body needs protein. A few protein foods, such as shrimps and lobster, are also considered negative Calorie foods. However, the list is restrictive and it would be difficult to stick to a diet based solely on these foods.

Eat to Reduce

It's been known since the 1940's that eating a little results in faster weight loss than starvation. So what about the low Calorie diets of 600 Calories a day? Want to ruin your metabolism, then go right ahead. Great idea. Stop yourself enjoying food for the rest of your life. But there's a window of hope here in combination with the **EATALL™** guide: spread those low Calories over a whole day and you could lose a lot of weight. Maybe you'll even use the bulkiest food for your buck to keep from being hungry – celery, cabbage, cucumbers… Do all foods beginning with 'c' have this wonderful characteristic? You know they don't: think chocolate. But, with the **EATALL™** way, you can increase the number of Calories you take in and enjoy other foods to spice up your life.

The Protein-only Diet

The best-known example of the protein-only diet is the **Atkins Diet**, launched in the seventies. Dr Robert C Atkins believed that eating sugar and carbohydrates is the cause of obesity, and controlling the amount of carbohydrates eaten would result in losing weight even though, over the same period of time, the Calories eaten might exceed the Calories taken in before starting the diet.

The first two weeks on the diet are strictly controlled. Only proteins, including meat, fish, poultry, eggs, dairy foods and fats are allowed. All fruit is prohibited, and only ¾ oz (20g) of carbohydrates from low glycemic vegetables, such as broccoli and cabbage, are allowed. The dieter then increases the amount of carbohydrates consumed until weight is no longer lost.

This diet undoubtedly works, but it does lead to a few problems: bad breath, constipation and, eventually, boredom. The first two weeks are terrible: eating a diet bereft of virtually all carbohydrates is an awful experience. It gets a little better after that, and you do lose weight. However, there may also be some health issues. Spread over the day the **EATALL™** way, however, this diet could possibly have even more potential, asuming you can overcome the other problems. Adding a few fun foods with the **EATALL™** way will definitely make the diet more interesting and probably enhance weight loss.

Food Combining

This method of weight control involves complicated computations detailing the amount of fiber, protein and carbohydrate in a particular meal, and how to combine them for that meal. This kind of diet can become a school science project rather than an attempt at weight control. If you can follow the books that have all the directions the mere extra energy you spend doing all that will also help you lose weight.

Weight Watchers

In this popular diet different foods are prescribed 'point values'. The dieter is given an individual number of points to stick to per day and may eat anything provided the total amount of food consumed during the day stays inside the daily limit. This means the dieter has to learn, or check, the number of points allotted to a particular food.

Weight Watchers™ is, perhaps, one of the diets where you learn to limit your eating with a specialized system. It becomes a part of your life to limit yourself to certain points. But who wants to do that for the rest of their life? Anyway, sometimes you simply get hungry for more because it's forbidden. Food isn't just in the body – the mind plays a powerful part in what, and how, we eat.

The Prescribed Menu

Maybe you prefer to stick to the same – potentially boring – menu every day? OK, you know the number of Calories, you get all the right proportions of food for your nutritional needs, you can have it all portioned out in your fridge. The **Banana and Milk Diet**, and the **Rice Diet**, are two well-known examples. You won't stick to whatever it is for more than two weeks, even if you've focused on chocolate. More likely it will become a way to rid yourself of chocolate cravings for ever, so that may be good!

Calorie Counting

Are you serious? The Calorie content of foods varies widely within the food group, and most people aren't that great at remembering long lists of numbers, or performing feats of mental arithmetic – especially when hungry. Added to that, many Calorie lists on food containers vary between Calories per weight (again variable) and Calories per serving (whatever that may be). Sure, this can work, even if it's just because you're using up extra Calories by simply doing the computations, but is this really a sensible, life-long regime for most people? However, if dieting this way appeals to you then go right ahead and combine it with the **EATALL™** way. You'll do even better and lose weight faster.

We don't actually suggest you *count* Calories when eating the
EATALL™ way, though we do suggest you keep some sort of check
on the portions you eat, that is we warn you not to increase your
normal Calorie consumption over the whole day. We've added a
variety of Calorie-approximated suggestions for **EATALL™**
portions at the end of the book. Keep roughly to the suggested
servings and you won't go far wrong.

The Cabbage Soup Diet

As mentioned in the **Catabolic Diet**, cabbage is a food which, in
the right quantities, will use more Calories to digest than it
makes available to the body. Therefore a low Calorie soup, based on
cabbage and low in fat and protein yet high in fiber, will certainly
jump-start weight loss.

This type of diet is not sustainable in the long run. Though it
undoubtedly is a quick weight loss diet used for, say, seven days,
eating prescribed foods every day, it soon becomes monotonous and
hard to stick to. It's also quite tricky to remember just what foods are
allowed on particular days of the diet. However, even when you
succeed with this diet you simply put the weight on again when you
stop!

The SugarBusters!™ Diet

Does the way our foraging ancestors ate give us clues for weight
loss? The **SugarBusters!™** diet is based on that premise. It
involves avoiding all simple sugars and all refined grains, including
wheat, rice, corn and rye.

There's no question that an excess of sugar in food is tricky for
the body to handle. Before the mass production of refined sugar

19

from sugar cane and sugar beet sweet food was limited to naturally sweet fruits and sweet vegetables. It took a fair number of those to ingest the amount of sugar in a candy bar or a soda, particularly in the northern climates where fruit tends to be tart. This diet is all about limiting the amount of sugar in your diet. Most people would agree that that's a good idea.

But it's not that easy to do, and many people last less than two weeks when they try such diets. What's great about the **EATALL™** way is that you can eat reasonable amounts of sugar in the same way that you can eat reasonable amounts of anything else. However, combining the **SugarBusters!™ Diet** with the **EATALL™** method is a great way to a trim figure.

The Slimming Tea Diet

B elieve it or not there are claims for a way to reduce simply by drinking a particular type of tea. Green tea is the most common suggestion, but there are also proprietary types of tea which are said to work even better. One brand, advertised to be the best, is sold for $50 (£25) for thirty teabags. If it were as simple as that we wouldn't have any weight problems, would we?

The Mediterranean Diet

T his diet is great for people living around the Mediterranean, and for those who have the time and love to cook. However, don't confuse this diet with general cooking around the Mediterranean. Pasta, for example, isn't exactly a slimming food. And remember there are some people living in the region who aren't actually known for their svelte figures.

What is fantastic about this region is that many Mediterranean countries serve appetizers. These have different names in the different countries: *tapas* in Spain, *hors d'oeuvres* in France, *mezethes* in Greece, *antipasta* in Italy, *meze* in North Africa. There is an impressive variation of dishes, all served in small portions. These are ideal for the **EATALL™** way. These tasty appetizers reflect the region's extraordinary bounty and reliance on seasonal produce. The main idea of the diet, based on these tidbits, is to have small portions of food – a common concept in many diets – but the Mediterranean diet still focuses on meals.

An interesting case in point is shown by those individuals who are used to home- cooked food in various countries – primarily from the nations with the highest life-expectancies in the world. Their citizens do not gain weight easily when living at home. They tend to eat small portions (by US standards, that is) of food over long periods of time. But, when those people come to live in the United States they, too, put on weight. They learn to gobble large portions of fast food (everything is bigger and faster, right?), just like everybody else. Those that don't are commonly found eating in local restaurants of their own country. It's when they return home that they again regain their natural figures. These findings support the fact that a lifestyle change is all that's needed; the diet itself may not matter that much, as long as the portions are reasonable and the eating more frequent.

The High Fiber Diet

The most famous high fiber diet, the **F-Plan Diet** by Audrey Eyton, prescribes eating high fiber foods instead of low fiber ones. However, it also prescribes a low Calorie intake. Many high fiber foods fill up the stomach with non-caloric ingredients. These foods also take longer to chew and digest, and therefore have a beneficial effect on elimination, so banishing constipation, a tiresome byproduct of some diets. High fiber foods may be a good food choice to follow, and should work well using the **EATALL™** way.

The Slim-Fast™ Plan & Similar Diets

The **Slim-Fast™** plan seeks to control weight by using carefully portioned meal and snack replacements. These 'meals' are manufactured to give a specific number of Calories together with the known nutrients the body needs.

In effect you buy tins or powders of carefully controlled servings (at a price) and turn your mealtimes into penances with what seem like small amounts of food. In some cases these food portions may not taste that great. It could put you off eating and, sometimes, that's exactly what it does. It also makes it more likely that you'll simply gulp down the food. Is that what you want? Can you really eat on such a plan for an extended period of time?

The Zone Diet

This particular diet, called **The Zone Diet** because it is carefully zoned between certain percentages, was created by Dr Barry Sears. It depends on a fixed percentage eating plan: 40 percent carbohydrate, 30 percent each of fat and protein. This requires a careful balance of the nutritional content of each meal. Quite possibly sound, but hard work to stick to.

The GI Diet

The Glycemic Index measures how quickly foods are broken down by the body to form glucose, the body's source of energy. High GI foods break down quickly and leave you longing for the next food fix. Low GI foods take longer to break down and leave you feeling satisfied for longer. Low GI foods are the essence of the diet. You follow a list of foods in a particular color zone. No doubt that's an excellent diet for all-round health, but it's still hard to follow. Even when you can buy the food at the store in ready made packs you may still have those nagging cravings for other foods. As with the **SugarBusters!™** diet, the **GI Diet** can be quite successful when combined with the **EATALL™** way

The Grapefruit Diet

This diet was at the height of its popularity in the 1980s. You eat grapefruit, or drink grapefruit juice, with every meal and this, magically, causes you to lose weight. Some people love grapefruit, but does that apply to everyone? And does it actually work?

Amazingly some research carried out at the Nutrition and Medical Research Center at Scripps Clinic in San Diego, USA, suggests that the simple act of adding grapefruit and grapefruit juice to your diet really can aid weight loss. Whether it can help you to shed sufficient pounds for your requirements is hard to say. But if you're a grapefruit fan, go for it. Half a grapefruit is a useful **EATALL™** portion.

Well, the list of diets you could adopt could go on for a very long time, but there's really no need. One thing is crystal clear. With diets the prohibitions are endless, and we all know where prohibitions lead.

Diets don't work for most people except for a short period of time. Some will take off weight initially; others fail after a few weeks. A very few will change their eating habits to be more healthy, and stick to a restricted diet for life. Most will try a diet and give up quickly – they don't have the time, they have cravings, or they simply don't like that way of getting their food requirements.

Most diets advocate a change in lifestyle which doesn't catch on – because the change they suggest isn't so much a change as a substitution: eat different food from the fattening kind. And what, exactly, is fattening food? Most food, in excess. What's more, most diets require that food to be served at special times of the day called 'meal times'. Children are forced to 'eat up,' though many of them balk at the idea only to have therapists infiltrate their lives. The majority will be dragooned into repeating the behavior that has made such a mess of their parents' lives. Why? Because the majority of us are hooked on the idea of eating 'meals'.

Politicians spout that 'the family which eats together stays together' as though, somehow, the food is a kind of glue. All it glues are rather large bodies into seats from which they're too heavy to move. There are many other things families can do to stay together – talk to each other, play games with each other, enjoy learning a new skill together. A little food, a little drink, and it fits right into the **EATALL™** way. What could be more fun for a family than sharing a few healthy snacks over a long period of time while playing a game or watching a movie? And sure, popcorn can be a great **EATALL™** portion.

President Bush said that he was in favor of family meals – as long as his mother wasn't cooking. Is that a clue? Fast food chains have worked out a way of serving food which turns it, in effect, into a kind of addiction so that home cooking no longer tastes good. Are we becoming fast food junkies? And that doesn't mean only eating fast, in fast food outlets. It means being unable to face a meal without that special brand of ketchup or mayo. It's been known for a long time that some pet foods contain additives that prove irresistible to pets. Is the same happening with our food?

The solution is simple. Change the times (both the number and the amount) of the way you eat your food and make each time you eat an **EATALL™** time.

THE SCIENTIFIC BASIS OF THE EATALL™ WAY

So, why does the **EATALL™** way work, even when you're targeting the loss of just those last few pounds? These, everybody knows, are the hardest of all to lose, for every one of us. And the **EATALL™** way will also work on those who have many more pounds to lose, even more than a hundred. How can this be? Well, before Richard explains what he thinks is going on, let's digress a little – not again, you groan.

Did you know that only about one in five diets has any scientific basis or support? Not that the word scientific should make you prick up your ears – it all depends on how well the experiment was performed, and whether the right 'controls' were present. Even then, you can always mess with the statistics to make things seem good. So, is my anecdotal story of any consequence? Are the tests by our friends sufficient to convince anyone, let alone you, the reader? Sure, it's nice to know that the **EATALL™** way works for some people, but should you spend your valuable time trying it out? The answer is yes. What a surprise I hear you say sarcastically… So let me explain why I'm sure it works.

First of all, I'll be able to show you that even if you don't lose waist or weight you'll be gaining great benefits for your body. You'll derive advantages such as lowering your cholesterol and insulin, as well as otherwise improving your general body biochemistry. Don't take my word for this – I'll illustrate this with others' experiments and measurements. I don't say that they did the experiments well or correctly, but the overall method is clear and supportive of what I'm advocating.

Secondly, it's evident that if you follow the **EATALL™** way you *will* lose weight and waist – more so if you're reducing the amount of food you actually ingest. Eating regularly each hour or so makes it easier to eat less as you don't have the problem with hunger.

A word of warning, however: if you cannot control how much you eat each time you eat, you'll have an even bigger problem and need to take action to ensure that you limit your food intake for each day to just enough for your body.

We've worked out several **EATALL™** portions, detailed later in the book, which will make it easier for you to judge the amount you should aim for each time you eat. That may take a little thought during the first few days, but eating these relatively small amounts at roughly hourly intervals will soon become second nature.

Eat Frequently to Lower Cholesterol

In 1964, a group from Czechoslovakia looked at the relationship between frequency of meals and their relation to overweight and metabolic effects. See Fabry et al., *The Lancet,* volume 2, pp 614-615. They studied a group of nearly four hundred men in their early Sixties and simply asked how often they ate. They measured various parameters, including body weight.

As the men described eating less frequently the amounts of extra weight, hypercholesterolemia and diminished glucose tolerance all increased. That was similar to results on a group of thirty to fifty year-olds who showed the same correlation even though those with the lowest number of meals ate fewer Calories. Notably, the study did not take snacks into account as much as 'meals'. The bottom line of this study is that it indicates a good correlation between eating more frequently and lowering the chance of being overweight and having high cholesterol.

Eat Frequently to Lower Insulin

In 1989, a Canadian group studied the metabolic advantages of increased meal frequency with what they referred to as 'nibbling' vs. 'gorging.' See Jenkins et al., *The New England Journal of Medicine,* volume 321, pp 929-934.

The group admitted that fifteen to twenty-five years before people were interested in altering the frequency of meals in order to study the effect on metabolism. They noted that having only one or two meals a day was associated with an increased cardiovascular risk. However, they concluded that: '... any clinical usefulness of increasing the frequency of meals for patients who were already overweight was offset by the failure to reduce the size of the meals. Consequently, the patients gained more weight because total caloric intake was increased. Consequently this approach to therapy wasn't explored further. A prohibition on eating between meals was advocated, especially in obese patients with diabetes.'

What this is saying is that they recognized that patients who ate more frequently, the ones who were eating snacks between meals, simply ate more food and thus put on weight. Not exactly a surprise.

However, they then went on to study the effect of seventeen 'snacks' consumed hourly, compared to three meals a day, running tests for a period of two weeks, with about three weeks between each test. Though only looking at seven men around forty years old they found that while body weight decreased slightly for both regimes (but not apparently in any significant manner), the amounts of bad cholesterol was significantly lowered by nibbling, and so were the levels of insulin and glucose.

Such a change in the blood cholesterol has long been known to be a factor in reducing the risk of cardiovascular disease. The above study states, however, that the use of increased meal frequency alone is not advocated, but that it may be beneficial when combined with diets with a low glycemic index and the like.

Eat Between Meals – Nibble!

These studies were summarized, among others, by Nancy Appleton Ph.D. – a clinical nutritionist and researcher – in a web article. She said that Mom was wrong and that 'nibbling is the best way to eat.' She noted that others had found that if food were eaten in the same amount but over a longer time period (that is eating smaller meals but more frequently) there would be weight loss as well as a reduction in cholesterol levels.

She added that eating more frequently resulted in a decline in appetite, and that in order to lose weight it seems wise to eat small meals. Those who reported that they ate more frequently were often those people who were thinner, more physically active, smoked less and drank less alcohol.

Free Living Trials Support Frequent Eating

In 2001, Titan et al., in the British Medical Journal, volume 323, pp 1-5, studied the frequency of eating and cholesterol levels in a group of people. Like the others discussed above they found that those who chose to eat more frequently had lower cholesterol levels than those who did not. The result is the same for such a 'free living' population as that found in short term trials in humans and animals under so-called laboratory conditions. Note that this result was obtained without regard to how many Calories were actually taken in – that is eaten.

Eat Less to Live Longer

We all know that it's healthier to eat less and thus not be heavier than the doctors recommend. Some even suggest that it's healthier to be below the average weight. For example, in 1985, the National Institute of Health, Centres for Disease Control, and the Department of Health and Human Services published a 'special report' stating: '[S]tudies based on life insurance data, the American Cancer Society Study and other long-term studies, such as the Framingham Heart Study and the Manitoba Study, indicate that weights associated with the greatest longevity tend to be below the average weights of the population as long as such weights are not associated with concurrent illness or a history of medical impairment.'

Studies on mice, where the poor things were fed lesser Calories (so called Caloric restriction (CR) diets), suggest that eating lesser amounts can have significant life expectancy benefits. Ian Williams Goddard, in an article published in November 2002, states:

'CR not only extends the lifespan of laboratory animals but also reduces the incidence of virtually all diseases of aging such as *cancer*, *heart disease*, diabetes, osteoporosis, *auto-immune disorders*, *neurological decline* and diseases such as *Alzheimer's* and *Parkinson's*.' [Citations omitted.] He urges that all animals tested, and thus by extension all humans, benefit in life and health with lower Calorie intake.

Don't Eat Junk

On that same website, www.mercola.com, a Dr. Joseph Mercola indicated support for eating more frequently, but mentioned that care is needed not to eat junk foods. The article concluded that: '[i]t will take some planning to provide the healthy snacks, but the rewards sure seem worth it.'

Smokers Benefit from Frequent Eating

In 1999, Powell et al. in J. Cardiovascular Risk, volume 6, pp 19-22, found that hospitalized smokers who said they ate more frequently had a lower risk of peripheral arterial disease and had lower cholesterol levels. Thus, there was potentially a benefit from eating between meals. They concluded that should such a result be confirmed for both smokers and non smokers this could be a good way to reduce the risk of cardiovascular disease in the Western world.

All in all, these studies and the associated commentary seem to support the idea of eating frequently, and in amounts that are preferably less than what would normally be consumed in the same time period. Of course, they all recommend eating the right kind of food, but even then the studies make clear that not only should you lose weight you'll also significantly alter your blood lipids, including cholesterol – thereby reducing your risk of cardiovascular disease.

So, does the **EATALL™** way have scientific basis? As you can see, the answer is clearly yes. It's not proven – to my mind it's impossible for anyone to prove anything in science except a negative – but we certainly get pretty close with the studies I mentioned and the anecdotal evidence of our own.

WHY DOES THE EATALL™ WAY WORK?

A Theory

Some of the scientists whose work I discussed above have theories on the History of Man. They talk about our ancestors grazing their food while the more modern way of eating is by gorging. They suggest that, when animals like man start gorging, there is an adaptive mechanism to store food – that is to lay down fat. They maintain that, by contrast, nibbling animals have a steadier metabolism.

These same scientists conclude that different types of animals have different enzymes active in their bodies, and that they therefore take in glucose, and form fat, in different ways. Titan et al. suggest that gorging in man leads to an increased risk of cardiovascular disease because of changes in the lipid profiles and in glucose metabolism.

Well, I have a Ph.D. and this certainly gives some weight to my scientific knowledge and ability. But does it actually qualify me to tell you how the **EATALL™** way works?

As it happens I studied molecular biology, not biochemistry. And yes, I used to teach biochemistry, but that was a long time ago. I know a bit about the body and its hormones, but only enough to be dangerous. You can read and accept all this if you wish – just don't rely on it to be scientific fact. But who actually *does* know enough about what is going on in the body to determine what really happens? That's it for the warning, and the philosophy.

Here is why I think the **EATALL™** way works:

One could simply say that the body does not like to be starved, and that having large meals means that there are periods of feast and then periods of famine. When the body is in famine mode and then takes in food it will use what is needed to survive, then store the rest

31

as fat. It will only build up protein very slowly (which is why it takes forever to gain weight by working out and building muscle mass) and the protein it takes in but cannot use at that time is simply excreted. Quite a waste, no pun intended, but that is why it's great to eat high protein foods: you get rid of the excess protein automatically. And if you don't get rid of it that means you're actually gaining muscle mass – what a fantastic story.

Now the sugars (carbohydrates, or so called 'carbs') are burned to generate the energy needed for the body to survive. A lot of that goes to the brain, which uses an extraordinary amount of energy. So keep right on thinking about becoming slim and burn up that carbohydrate food. But, the sugars that *aren't* burned will get converted to fat.

Now fat is not that bad in small amounts – we all need some. It's the little extra 'padding' around the waist and thighs that we all seem to object to. Our society objects to it, but not all cultures take the same view. There are actually those that like this type of figure. Clearly another way to be happy with one's figure is simply to move to those locations. Who knows whether that's healthy – but the term healthy is a moveable feast (got to love the puns) as those in the know seem to change their minds all the time.

One example of just such a change is when X-rays were first discovered. Everyone thought it was healthy to have their picture taken and even to spend some time catching those rays. Now we think (or do we know) that that isn't such a great idea.

Another example is the storage of wine in bottles. You've always been told to store them horizontally, right? Because then the liquid stops the cork from drying out? California wine-growers know this is nonsense – you can store wine bottles in any way you like or that's convenient – even stand them upright. It's the humidity outside the sealed bottles that keeps the corks hydrated. Another sacred myth which is no longer sacred.

And what about the sun's rays so many of us have spent time soaking up? Now the skin cancer people recommend otherwise. Turning from pale beige to a tan color is apparently not as 'healthy' now as we used to think. All the same, many people ignore this advice, and some people even suggest that *some* sun protects against cancer because that's the way to get your dosage of vitamin D.

My point is that theories aren't always right, and it takes a long time for the collective unconscious to change. Anyway, I digress – but at least it's more interesting that way, right?

Now when the body is in feast mode it might or might not store fat. This will really depend on the level of that tricky hormone insulin, as well as several others in the body. Diabetics generally have trouble controlling insulin levels and a lot of harm can be done to their bodies because of this. They tend to be overweight, have eye problems and may die prematurely. Consequently, many diets try to regulate the amount of insulin.

The **SugarBusters!™** diet, for example, is one I kind of like. It suggests you keep the amount of simple sugars in the food low so that you don't trigger insulin surges. Such sugars include glucose (common sugar), lactose (present in milk and many fruits), fructose (also in many fruits) and the like. More complex sugars do not have this effect and are encouraged in that diet – hence the recommendation for whole grain foods which, because they're not refined, tend to have low simple sugar levels.

Yes, the body will eventually break down those complex sugars into simple ones, but without such a great affect on the amount of insulin in the body. If insulin is high it will cause sugars to be converted into fat. Without such a high level of insulin the fat conversion will be significantly reduced.

This has been known for a long time of course, so I'm not telling you anything you wouldn't immediately agree to having heard or read about already.

But let's ponder that thought. How do we keep insulin low? Better still, how do we prevent insulin spikes, that is times when the level of insulin is raised, briefly, and then reduced?

In healthy humans such spikes may be regulated by the body without any problems, but in diabetics they're not so well regulated. And a spike in the level of insulin means a higher likelihood of storing more fat.

What this is actually telling us is that eating the **EATALL™** way is not only extraordinarily helpful to diabetics, it is actually likely to be a factor in the prevention of the disease for those of us who do not have any symptoms yes, but might develop them in the future..

Diabetes and the EATALL™ Way

In the studies discussed above it was clear that frequent eating kept insulin and glucose from spiking. I discussed this issue with a friend of mine who is diabetic but doesn't take insulin. He has to be careful what he eats, but right now doesn't have to inject artificial hormones into his body. He does, however, carefully record and monitor his blood glucose, and tries to ensure that it's within a suitable range.

He's a little overweight (I have to admit to that even though I know he's going to read this), but he didn't have easy access to a scale to weigh himself on. When following the **EATALL™** way he quickly found that his glucose level became steady. No longer did it go up and down all the time with meals, it simply stayed flat-lined. That was great for his body, some might even say healthy, as it meant that the insulin in his body was probably level too. He slowly noticed that he felt lighter and indeed soon determined that his pants no longer fit him. He was losing waist! Clearly this supported what is said above. Even in a body that is having some issues with its relationship to insulin the method appears to work.

Now, do we really care about this? Consider that a recent article indicated that you're at a higher risk of getting diabetes if you have more than ten points on its system. Simply being older than sixty-five gave you nine points, and if anyone in your family had or has diabetes that's enough to score you the ten. So, yes, I think we do care. Just being older means the chance of diabetes increases. However, the disease is now also affecting younger people, more of them every year. Tragically statistics show that even children are being affected by diabetes.

If we were to be able to reduce the chance of getting diabetes – and, believe me, you don't want to get this disease or condition, particularly if you don't like needles – then using the **EATALL™** way should help prevent the onset of this disease. The body will be under less stress and, it would appear, less likely to have issues with its hormones. Allowing the body to communicate better with those hormones makes it, and us, happy and content.

How Frequently and How Much should you Eat?

We're often asked how often and how much does one have to eat. The answer is unfortunately complex, but also quite simple. The simple answer is about every hour, about one seventeenth of the total food you would normally eat in a day.

The more complex answer is to eat often, and to eat sufficient food so that you don't get hungry – but at the same time only consume in a day the same as, or less than, you used to eat (or should eat according to your medical adviser). How you space the timing and the amounts is up to you and your schedule. However, you need to avoid meal-size portions and long gaps between eating. You can afford to have a space of two hours every now and then – but try to avoid doing it too often.

You can also enjoy a full meal every now and then – just not that often. The amount you eat at a sitting can be varied to keep it interesting for you, as can the timing. Many times that you eat you may well just have a quick bite – possibly not the most healthy way to eat, but a lot better than the alternative. Many times it may just be a few crackers or some cheese – again, this is perfectly fine as long as you try to keep a balance of what you already know to be healthy food in any one day. You'll be surprised how quickly your tastes will change – eating half an apple instead of a doughnut, for example. Your body will automatically respond to the healthier food when you give it time to consider what you're taking in, slowly and deliberately.

By now we're sure you understand that the body will lose waist (who cares about weight when clothing size is reduced?) if it believes that it's not starving and that there's no need to store fat. Spurring your body to lose the stored fat is the next trick. There's a delicate balance between feast and famine. Staying away from feasting or gorging is not enough, we have to stay away from famine, too. So the answer is to eat often enough, and to eat sufficient food to keep your body healthy, as well as to take in whatever you believe your body needs to ensure it's fully nourished.

One way to do this is simply to work out what you're recommended by nutritionists for three meals a day. Then eat that amount over the course of the whole day. That way you're getting everything you need in a daily fashion and distributing it over the course of the day. Of course we know that's not really practical; no one cooks or prepares that many meals in a day. We discuss ways of easily achieving **EATALL™** portions later in this book.

But you get the idea. Simply work out what is the equivalent for keeping your body nourished in quantity and quality. You'll find that you actually eat less than that anyway and, if you're like us, you'll 'cheat' all the time by eating things you know you shouldn't. That helps keep you happy and your body really won't mind.

The whole secret of adapting to the **EATALL™** way is to keep it interesting and fun. Most people like to munch on junk food, or chocolates and candies – it makes them happy. If you're happy you can eat that way for as long as you like, just try to make sure you keep the amounts in check and eat healthy food as well. It will become a life-long way of eating and keeping healthy.

The simple solution is to eat a small portion of food every hour so that you don't get hungry. The secret is to eat *small* portions of food – make sure you're not just going out for those Mac attacks and stuffing them down your throat.

If in doubt have a portion that you think is too small. If you're still hungry, have another such portion fifteen to twenty minutes later. As time goes by you'll be able to lengthen the period between such portions, but try not to go without *some* food for longer than an hour. We will give you a number of ideas for **EATALL™** portions later in the book. These will make it easy for you to adopt the **EATALL™** way

Eating Fruit the EATALL™ Way

So, are we saying you should avoid fruit because it has too much sugar? Not really, just be aware that most fruit is simply sugar and water, not that much different from a soda. But it has lots of vitamins and fiber too, which is good. Just try to choose the right fruit. Know that if you eat watermelon you're basically putting pure sugar into your body. Pineapple does the same thing. The advantage of pineapple is the roughage, but you'll have a high insulin spite, a big price to pay for the pleasure.

Vegetables, on the other hand, generally don't create those issues. While carrots and sweet corn have a high sugar content and you need to be careful how much of them you eat, the green and deeply colored vegetables are just great. So, don't think you cannot eat all fruit and all vegetables, just eat small amounts of the sugar-laden ones and as much as you want of the others.

Drinking the EATALL™ Way

Drinking fits equally well into this method. Preferably water, but any drink will do as long as you understand that diet sodas have lots of salt in them (not good for your heart and blood vessels) and that regular sodas are full of those horrid simple sugars – you're actually better off eating a candy bar than drinking those sugar-laden drinks. If you must drink them do so slowly as you're playing chicken with your insulin levels.

Even drinking so-called healthy fruit juices does practically the same thing. That glass of orange juice in the morning is pure sugar to your system. People always say it's different from other sugars as it's natural. We beg to differ. Sugar is simply sugar and the body will react with insulin. It's true that orange juice is a good choice from a vitamin C point of view; just be sure to drink it in small amounts, or drink a larger amount over a longer period of time, or dilute it with some water.

A small glass of vegetable juice can be an excellent **EATALL™** portion, but be cautious even here. Some commercial vegetable juices have added sugar. And carrot juice is naturally sweet. As always, read the labels and adjust your **EATALL™** drink portion accordingly.

Alcoholic drinks are fine too. Don't get us wrong here, we're not suggesting you become an alcoholic or anything. Those drinks have sugar in them as well as alcohol, and they *can* raise insulin levels. But if you drink them over a reasonable time period there won't be a problem. They help maintain the 'food' levels in your body just like the solid stuff. They're useful when you're concerned about whether you ate recently or not.

Are we saying alcohol is good for you? Not exactly. But a glass of wine every now and again can be an excellent **EATALL™** portion.

Cheating in an EATALL™ Way

Is that really cheating? We don't think so. We tell ourselves that if we like a particular food we can have it – we just remind ourselves to make sure that we only eat a reasonable amount if at all possible. It rarely is, but perhaps that's just us. We simply get ourselves to eat that food over a longer period of time. We don't allow the body to know the whole of what is being consumed and just deal with it in a ho-hum way.

If you ate a whole pound of chocolate at once (OK, for us it's usually two pounds) the body might just notice, right? But if you eat that same chocolate over a twenty-four hour period the body just keeps chugging away.

No, this isn't suggesting that you do this. It's an extreme example. We're just maintaining that the body can accommodate a lot of silly or poor eating habits provided it isn't stuffed at one sitting.

The challenge is to make those new habits into something the body won't notice. Remember when you were a kid (or, for many of us, always) and you were trying to get away with something? This is the same thing. You know you want that dessert. You know if you eat it all at once the body will know and it will be mean to you – read, it will store it as fat. But if you hide it among other foods and slip a little bit in every now and then, voila, the parental unit is fooled and you got away with it.

Does that mean you can never blatantly say boo to the body? Of course we're not saying that. Even when you're eating according to the **EATALL™** way you may still get those urges. OK, OK, you *will* get those urges. Don't worry, the body won't punish you too badly.

Maybe more like a rap on the knuckles than a big spanking.

The solution is to try to eat as often as you can – that is every thirty to sixty minutes. Just grab hold of something, small or even a little more substantial if you like. You want to aim to keep the hunger pangs away at all times so that you simply won't even miss having a meal. Naturally, you or your boss will love this as all of a sudden you can finish a workday in less time than before because you don't have to take time out for a meal.

The amount you eat depends on your present weight, your body type, your fitness level, your metabolism and your feelings. These will change with time when you are eating the **EATALL™** way, in the same way that your age changes with time – inevitably.

Eat Slowly

Learn to eat slowly. By that we mean take your time over each mouthful, savor the food, chew well for food that needs it – that is, anything solid – but don't forget to hold it in your mouth for some time. This not only brings out the tastes and textures to their full extent, it also activates digestion even before the food reaches your stomach. You'll enjoy the food more, you'll discover tastes you never knew existed, and this way of eating also cuts down on the quantities you eat without your even being aware of it. Ideally it's part of eating frequently – the **EATALL™** way.

It sounds strange at first, but holding liquid food in your mouth, beer and wine for instance, also increases their taste, and so the pleasure you derive from them. Wine tasters have long known this, but it works equally well with fruit and vegetable juices – even with water.

The reports mentioned above clearly correlate spreading the consuming of your food throughout the day with lowered cholesterol levels – quite a nice trick, really, since the same amount of cholesterol was presumably entering via the diet, the genetics of the people was the same, and no drugs were being used. This same report also noted a decline in insulin and indicated that the weight of the people was reduced when they ate more often. Clearly this is great support for what we're suggesting. While those in the 'know' advocate that you eat a well-rounded snack – or a so-called 'healthy' snack and no junk food – that may be hard to do in reality. And maybe it doesn't actually matter that much what you eat, or precisely when you eat. You don't want to be a slave to timing. Just keep eating **EATALL™** portions throughout your waking hours.

Of course there's no need to cook or prepare fifteen to seventeen meals a day. Unless you're in the army or in jail, or paid a healthy sum to do so, you'll never agree to such a regime. However, eating a small amount frequently, and occasionally having a more substantial bite to eat, is quite manageable. That way of eating should have the same positive results as indicated in the tests cited above.

We haven't performed any biochemical analysis, and know of no other than the ones already mentioned above. Is there a positive side to this? You bet. Anyone can readily guess or even study what is going on here – we can measure glucose, insulin and other parameters and can draw correlations. But the bottom line is: we can all lose waist with the **EATALL™** way, we can all feel better and get more time for our usual activities. We can also simply spend more time at meals – that is, eating. What did we just write?

Right: spend more time at each meal. Don't look on those eating occasions as meals, rather they're simply a series of closely connected **EATALL™** portions eaten over closely connected **EATALL™** times.

We're saying eat all the time. That means if it a meal takes three hours, like in Paris or Rome, great. In that time, you can eat at least three **EATALL™** portions. That's all part of the package. Why do you think many Europeans are still relatively slender? They eat well (except perhaps us Brits) and look great. The same holds for the Japanese. The people in those nations love to take their time over meals. They eat small portions. They talk a lot and are energetic. They have fun. It's all part of the **EATALL™** way.

So go ahead, enjoy a meal, and just don't rush it. Don't let your body see all the food at once; convince it that it's happy with what you're doing. The occurrence of a meal is simply part of the overall plan to keep eating throughout the day.

CASE HISTORIES

We can't provide all the stories and anecdotes we've come across here. What follows is just a small 'tasting' for your enjoyment. What we have tried to do is carefully choose very different stories: A man working in the office all day, an older woman who has always had problems controlling her weight, a man who combined the **EATALL™** way with considerable physical exercise, and finally a man suffering from diabetes. This last is perhaps the most telling story of all; it is clear that many diabetics could improve their physical condition by using the **EATALL™** way, even if they are injecting insulin.

The method described in this book has been successfully applied by many other people; they all used their own interpretations. The **EATALL™** way can be adapted to most life styles – you'll readily be able to make it fit into your life. And the rewards aren't simply a smaller waist and disappearing love handles. Your energy will increase and your health will improve.

Richard's Story

OK, so I didn't start off exactly fat or even overweight, but my doctor suggested that I should lose a couple of pounds and get down to 168lb. I was at 172lb and was to remain there for several years.

I know he was just joking, or at least I thought so. I'm six foot tall and, while having some love handles, wasn't otherwise carrying too much extra weight. My identical twin weighed at least ten pounds more than I did so I felt fine.

But there was this nagging challenge. I was going to rise to it. I decided I'd would work out more regularly, even become someone who worked out almost every day. OK, sometimes that meant I only looked at the machines, but I did actually get on them at least weekly. I ended up joining a club and went there religiously for a few months – until I couldn't stand the sport programs they insisted on showing on *all* the television screens.

I read about diets: **Atkins, SugarBusters!™** and the like. I even tried out some but without success. Yes, I would get down to 168 lb but it would never last. One big meal and I was above 172 lb again. It was frustrating and depressing. I returned to my regular habit of one meal a day at dinner time, with chocolate periodically – but of course that doesn't count.

Then I read a book about Japanese women never getting fat – at least until they ate American food. Small portions were the main rationale but that is no good as a method on its own because you still get hungry between meals. Then I saw an advertisement about five meals a day. I knew that was going to be tough – how could anyone possibly cook that often? I have little time for meals.

At that point my old science background came back to me. Yes, of course. You need to start burning up fat. OK, I know that sounds like a 'duh' moment but it was more than that. I recalled that insulin is a great hormone to have around, but you must control it. Diabetics put on weight because they lose control of insulin. But if you control it you can have it be a great friend. It can actually cause fat to be burned rather than to be deposited.

My existing regime was ideal for storing fat. My body saw food once a day. It was in starvation mode. It saw food and said let's store that, because it didn't know when it would see food again.

So it occurred to me that I needed to eat more to lose weight. In fact I needed to eat all the time. Even chocolate could become a really helpful part of my diet – finally. It could be part of my no-meal plan. No longer would I be wedded to meals, but on waking until sleeping I would simply eat. No more actual meals, I'd simply be snacking throughout the day.

Everyone I mentioned this to said 'Oh, yes, I always graze too.' But none of them were losing weight. In fact most of them were at least a little overweight. *They forgot to forget meals.*

Society is so into meals people forget that it's just a convenience and a social event. What I'm talking about is taking in food – whatever food you like but in small amounts, every thirty to sixty minutes. It can just be a couple of crackers or, better still, chocolate or meat or fish. Whatever. So I thought, right – I might as well try it.

I bought some tasty crackers like Trisquit™ and WheatThins™, a few chocolate-covered pretzels, concentrating on finding snacks that were low in sugar. My thought process was that if I was going to have sugar I was going to eat it in a really tasty form – like chocolate or candy – and yes, it was part of what I would eat. Then I started eating that way. It was really easy to just keep food at my desk, in the car and in a pocket. I would eat very small amounts and didn't see a 'meal' for a couple of days.

At that point I weighed myself. I had lost weight. I was down to 170 lb! I felt great. I was never hungry. I kept going for several more days. People noticed I wasn't really eating, but I had no dinner commitments at the time, so I just carried on with my experiment. I worked out less during this time as I was busy on other projects. In four more days I was down to 168 lb!

Then I had to have a meal with a friend. I was nervous. Would my weight just go back up? We had a great time with plenty to eat and drink. Yes, I even tried alcohol with the new plan. The next day I had lost even more weight. Down to 167 lb. Wow, I thought – this is great, I lose weight even when I eat more food.

After that I was off out of town. Lots of meal commitments, but I just ate half at most of whatever was there – and kept on snacking all the time. On the plane I kept Trisquit™ crackers nearby. I never got hungry and so even with food in front of me it was easy to stop eating. That was new for me. I usually have a 'see food diet'. When I see food I eat. No more.

I didn't weigh myself for a couple of days but I was getting worried about my pants. They were obviously getting old and not fitting anymore. It never occurred to me that my body was the problem.

When I got back, now two weeks into my experiment, I was down to 160 lb. I couldn't believe it. Surely that can't be right? I must have a faulty scale. I went to find another one – a fancy one. And yes, I was down to 160 lb. Better still, I was at 14% body fat, down from a rather high 18%.

Wow! That meant pretty much all the weight I'd lost was from fat loss. Working out wasn't the cause since I hadn't had time to do a lot of that.

I was pleased with myself and I felt great. It was no big deal for me to stick with the continuous eating. I loved the fact that I lost more weight when I had a big meal. So now I got serious. I weighed myself throughout the day to see what was going on. I took care to collect relevant data. At the same time I drank a lot of water as I live in a desert. Well OK, San Diego, but it's very dry there.

Actually I was in Maui for a few days. I would get up in the morning and go for a jog, shower and weigh myself. Before the jog I would weigh about 162 lb, then 160 lb after I got back. Throughout the day I would increase in weight until by bedtime I might weigh in at about 164 lb. This pattern repeated for a few days. I'd reached a plateau.

That was fine by me. I was way under what I'd aimed for. I was actually 8 lb under, and 14% fat seemed good to me too. So I went back to San Diego happy and decided to visit the tailor. I had lost 2.5 inches off my waist. I now had a smaller waist measurement than when I was at university. No wonder my pants were falling down. It cost me a fortune to have them all taken in but I loved it.

That was the point at which I decided to buy new ones as I really wanted to buy some with 31 in waist labels. I had to get new shirts too, of course. My tummy was now tight and I had a six pack. This was a first for me. I'd tried everything before this time. Even sit-ups, and we all know how tough those are. But here I am, staring in the mirror, not even flexing (oh, well, just a touch then) and there were the ripples. Wow, I was pleased.

So, two weeks on and nothing new to report; just the same data and all was good. My friends thought me crazy but had to admit to the facts. So I wondered how to spread the word.

Then it happened. My body decided we had not done enough. All of a sudden, after about six weeks into the regime, my pants were no longer fitting. No, I hadn't gained weight – I'd actually lost more. Miraculously, I was down to 155 lb. My pants needed another half inch taken in. And when I worked out I felt lighter. My running was much faster. OK, I still took twenty-five minutes to run five kilometers, but that was really good for me. What it meant was that I hadn't reached a plateau earlier on. I'd just found a second tier. And my fat content was down to 12%.

This is a great method. My body had, in effect, lost thirty years and I had greater energy and high spirits. I was delighted, and had discovered the **EATALL™** way to lose weight.

I was still drinking a little alcohol (hence the high spirits) when my friends were around. I had large meals occasionally. I ate chocolate. I ate ice cream. There wasn't anything I couldn't eat. I just ate all the time.

I saw my doctor and he noticed right away how much weight I'd lost. I told him it was his fault. He was impressed. He concurred that what I was doing was healthy. My body mass index (BMI) was healthy.

Other people I met thought I looked too thin. I think that was mainly that they wished they looked like me but weren't sure they could get to the same point. That's when I challenged them to try the **EATALL™** way for themselves, and you can read a few of their stories on the following pages. The main point is that they all had success. This was great.

Now, two months into the method, I'd lost 18 lbs and 6% body fat. I ate whatever I wanted all the time and never got hungry. I was traveling like crazy yet still able to keep it up. When I was with people who ate meals I kept up with them and just snacked or drank fun drinks between meals, including Pina Colada. I was exercising regularly and people noticed I was slim.

After a few months I had my cholesterol levels checked. I've had a history of high cholesterol for the last few years. I'd tried changing my diet in that time and even exercising more but that failed to work. I was put on medicine to lower it. It went down to the high end of normal. But, by eating the **EATALL™** way, it went down well into normal – over 15% lower, and my ratio of good to bad cholesterol sky rocketed. Needless to say, my doctor wasn't just impressed, he was surprised. He even started talking of taking me off the medicine.

A Nibbler's History

After being sent the prologue of this book I sensed immediately that this was a method I could follow successfully. Actually, I didn't think Richard really needed to take off any weight, he looked fine to me, so I was even more impressed that the **EATALL™** way worked for him. However, he's not only twenty-eight years younger than me, he's a man, and men slim more easily than older women. Not because their metabolism is intrinsically faster, but because they speed theirs up by being more active physically and, generally, have a larger body to support.

I've had a checkered weight history. I've always found it difficult to lose weight, so I think I'm a useful example for this book.

I was an overweight teenager. I wanted to slim, but had no idea how to go about it. I'm not sure I even correlated the amount I ate with the amount I weighed. But I did discover a small book called *Eat to Reduce*, by Dr Victor Lindlahr. This diet was based on what he called 'catabolic' foods that have a minus caloric value, that is the body uses more Calories to digest the food than are actually in the food. The diet also advocated eating only 600 Calories a day. There's no question one loses weight on that diet, but it does nothing to allay hunger pangs. I stuck to it for a week, then found I was too hungry to carry on.

Meanwhile I got engaged. It so happened that the man I was going to marry had to be abroad for three months. How wonderful if he came back to a slim me! While he was away I dug out my Lindlahr book, determined on a svelte figure for the wedding.

It worked, but more by good luck than anything else. It so happened that I walked to and from work – a round trip of about three miles – twice daily. I kept to the diet for mealtimes but couldn't resist an 8 oz bar of Nestles milk chocolate additionally every day, nibbled at intervals. I did resist serious inroads into the cookies I

46

baked for our wedding reception, though I nibbled on the results – just to make sure they tasted right. In fact I was eating the **EATALL™** way without having any idea what I was doing.

And I lost weight – thirty pounds of weight. I didn't even realize it was happening until my girlfriends gave me a 'shower' and my party dress was so big I couldn't wear it. I was using the Lindlahr diet, yes; but I was eating chocolate (my big addiction) and nibbling cookies as well. I never understood why I lost weight that way. Now I realize it worked because, unknowingly, I was eating the **EATALL™** way.

I weighed 112 lb when I married, and I looked fantastic. I continued to stay slim through the birth of my children, including twins. It wasn't till some years after my husband died that weight began to creep up again. Instead of the 112 lb when I married, I weighed in at 147 lb. That's definitely too heavy.

That's when I decided to give Richard's method a go. I lost 15 lb without too much trouble – and without hunger pangs.

I lose weight fairly slowly on any diet, or by any method. The **EATALL™** way, perhaps combined with Lindlahr's catabolic food system or some other diet of choice, should make it painless for anyone to lose weight. What Lindlahr did not spell out, but what is obvious to me now, is that catabolic foods are only catabolic in small amounts. Eat large portions of such foods and they're potentially as fattening as any other source of food. What's useful about them is that, for the most part, they combine bulk with low Calories. That helps provide the feeling of fullness my body is always going on about.

The point, of course, is to eat frequently, and to keep the portions small. That, in essence, is what I did to lose weight in the first place, and what I do now to lose weight. It's easy, it's healthy and I can stick with it for the rest of my life.

A Dancer's Story

I lost 25% of my weight: eating the **EATALL™** way, and I enjoy my reflection in the mirror every day.

I met Richard at a dance studio. I weighed over 240 lbs at a height of only 5 ft 10 ins. I was intrigued by the **EATALL™** method he suggested I consider adopting. I used it in combination with the dance lessons which I'd just started. I was learning to be an instructor and decided to enter dance competitions with my new dance partner. The result of combining the dancing with the **EATALL™** way was amazing.

I'd been significantly overweight throughout most of my life. Now it feels terrific to have finally taken off the weight for good with this great new **EATALL™** method. I'd heard a lot about plans that have people eating six or seven small meals a day; it always sounded absurd to have to stop my day so many times for such a tiny meal. Before, just like everybody else, I was eating whatever sounded good and had no regard for my body or the stress I was putting it through. Now, after eating the **EATALL™** way, I feel so much more relaxed, at ease, and self confident for the first time in many years.

The way the **EATALL™** method worked for me was that, instead of having so many meals a day, I just cut the amount I ate at meals and continued to snack on small healthy quantities of food throughout the day. It became very convenient and easy to grab a couple of bites at a time, yet still be able to continue on with my day.

Lots of dancing and the continuous snacking were keeping my metabolism burning all day and helped me drop sixty pounds in six months. It was incredible to wake up on certain days and notice such a huge change in my body. Previously it had always been so hard to regulate my diet and to keep to the different exercises.

Continuing to snack and at the same time having the choice to eat whatever I wanted was a great feeling. It's all about moderation and maintaining control over how much your body needs to ingest. Many people continue to think that without several large meals a day they will not get the nutrients they need. The truth is the body only needs around 2000 Calories (for a man of my size) to keep it healthy, energetic, and in shape. The **EATALL™** way does wonders for those willing to take the step and try a new approach to eating. No more large meals and overwhelming Calorie consumption; just steady snacking of more healthy food than junk and it will do wonders for your weight loss.

Of course, I think that the exercise I was doing also helped me lose weight faster. Even so, the result of combining the **EATALL™** method with dance was almost unbelievable. Moderation and control are the key variables for this amazing method. Willpower; and mind over body, are also very important. You need to want to change your body, and to have the determination to succeed, in order to do what it takes to get used to the change.

After some time your body will no longer need to ingest so many Calories for you to feel full. At first it will be odd getting used to the small quantities, but the reward will be one for a lifetime. Without this life changing experience it would have been very difficult for me to accomplish this marvelous change. It's one I'll never regret and I smile about it every day.

A Diabetic's Story

I found that eating the **EATALL™** way, that is every hour to hour and a half, raised my blood sugar readings to start with, up to the high end of the control readings. This was due to the time at which I had to take a reading. Sometimes I had to do it within one hour of eating; the reading is always higher in that timeframe for everybody. However, after adjusting to this, my blood sugars were consistently in the middle part of the range. The control range is 70 - 120 mg/dL, whereas I checked in at the 80 - 100 mg/dL range while using the **EATALL™** way.

Before using the **EATALL™** method my readings were all over the place, some were even as high as 150 - 170 mg/dL. I did have several in the normal range, but not as consistently as after eating the **EATALL™** way.

I was also able to lose 10 lb in a roughly two-week time frame by eating frequently. What's more I kept the weight off for the whole three months I was following the **EATALL™** way. I didn't feel hungry at any time, and I found that I neither wanted nor needed a big meal in the evening. Previously I'd needed large portions to last me through the night.

The only time I had any problems was remembering to eat every hour or so at work. I felt that once my body had adjusted to the schedule it worked just fine for me and I certainly think it would work for others.

GRAZING THE EATALL™ WAY

Everyone we talk to maintains they already know about this 'grazing' method. But they don't. If they did know they would all be doing it – which they aren't.

While grazing is very close to the **EATALL™** way it still allows for full meals. Grazing or, as we prefer to say, snacking the **EATALL™** way, cuts out large meals; it's a method that can be easily followed. It is, in fact, a change in your way of life. No longer are you bound to those meal times. No longer do you have to cook those meals. You can now eat when convenient while always keeping food (or drink) in your body. You'll never *need* to eat, but you'll do so frequently and on your terms. Many young people already do this; unfortunately an unprecedented number are becoming obese because they buy large portions of takeaways, not realizing they could save their money – and their waists – if they shared the small-size portions with a friend, or even two.

What does it mean to be full?

Have you ever been told you have to stop eating when you're full? Do you assume your body knows when you're full, and that being full is a good thing? Does your body really have any idea what amount of food you have in there?

Not at all, this feeling is a purely physical switch. You could have a hundred Calories in there, or two thousand, depending on the food intake, and on how much and what you drank. The point is your body has no idea. It's merely saying OK, I cannot fit any more in there. It's not saying that's good, you did great, just the right amount, thanks very much. It doesn't know anything except that it gives you a sensation of fullness, and for some over-indulged bodies even that feeling doesn't function any more.

51

With the **EATALL™** guide you can get your body to help you. As you put less food *at a time* into your stomach it will gradually shrink. You'll feel full even when you've eaten quite a small amount. You'll keep that feeling by getting your body used to having small amounts of food around all the time. That way you're in control, not your body. You're saying you're going to eat even though you're not feeling hungry. You're saying you've had enough even when the body doesn't say you're full.

The body is only adapted to tell you about extremes: starvation or satiation. Either you've had nothing to eat for a long time or you've had a binge. So for extremes you're in good shape. It's just the body saying enough already. But if you get into the habit of constantly putting food into your body, you're telling it, OK keep the machinery going, don't slow down, burn this up and then I'll give you more. The metabolism becomes 'live' – and we can promise you that you'll notice the difference. You'll finally be the one in control.

Forget nagging mothers who tell you to clean your plate – eat what is the right amount to eat, not what someone else thinks is right. Regrettably, most mothers have no idea. They're just acting historically, repeating what their mother, their mother's mother, and the mother before that handed down as holy writ. Your body can tell you when you step out of line; otherwise be wise and in control.

Sumo Wrestlers

Do you know how Sumo wrestlers get to look the way they do? Do you want to look like them? True, they're considered handsome in some societies, but what if you don't buy into that? It's strictly your choice. Want to be like them, put on that much weight and get that great low body mass center? Then go ahead, eat one enormous meal a day. Binge on that meal. Gobble up lots of fat and protein and carbs. Then starve yourself the rest of the day. Work out as much as you want.

That way you'll gain plenty of weight. Why? The body is starving. It will store the food as soon as it can as it doesn't know when its next meal will be coming from, or when it will get food again.

Fat is the easiest way to store food, so there goes the waistline. Thighs are great places to put that fat, too. So feel free, if you want a big waist and huge thighs eat like those athletes do. If not, then think about your body. Tell it that you'll feed it all the time, so chill out, burn the food and don't worry because more is on the way.

That way you don't need to plan for the starvation phase of the day, you don't need to store that fat. In fact, you can persuade the body to go ahead and burn some of that stored fat now. What you're doing is making your body a promise that if you didn't give it enough this time, more is on the way.

Who can use the EATALL™ way?

There are no limits on who can use this method. There are some case histories for heavy people as well as those who want to lose that last ten pounds. It's harder for relatively slim people to lose weight, yet this method trims even slim bodies effortlessly. You can imagine how much easier it is for those with a few more pounds to lose.

All the evidence that exists supports this method. Just a brief look at all the diets discussed above, and a brief scan through the many diet books available, shows that you'll lose weight if you eat smaller portions more slowly and more frequently. The scientific studies discussed above have shown this to be a truth.

The only question then is this: can you get used to the method? Those who simply try it out and give up after a few days are going to be disappointed. You need to think of the **EATALL™** way as a lifestyle change rather than something you do for a few weeks and then go back to your old way of eating. Look on it as a true commitment. This is *not* a diet, that is to say a discipline which allows you only certain foods and seems always to be fighting your body and those insistent cravings. Not in the least – the **EATALL™** way is a method where you simply don't feel hunger, you automatically eat small amounts, you're never dissatisfied with the food and you can readily adapt to any circumstance.

What you have to do is to reset your brain, your expectations and the history of meals. This book helps you with ideas on how to do that. You'll come up with plenty more of your own which will make the **EATALL™** way work for you. Commit to getting control of your body and don't let others in fast-food chains or large portion serving restaurants, ruin your figure – and quite possibly your life.

Why will eating the EATALL™ way work?

The main reason is psychological. Instead of being told not to eat, the method encourages you to eat – often. This means that one of the main stumbling blocks of diets – the *don't* commands: *don't eat*, or *don't eat this type of food*, no longer apply, and consequently the psychological negative is not brought to bear. That's a great relief.

There's still a proscription – *eat small amounts, but do eat.* That isn't nearly as damaging as constantly stopping yourself from eating. On the contrary, the next bit of food is only a short half-hour to an hour away. The hunger gripes simply will not appear, you can vary the food, you can even use 'bad' food. It's up to you.

And, though this isn't a Calorie-controlled method, the amounts of food suggested for each **EATALL™** time are small. The size is up to you, but you'll automatically eat less as long as you take your time. Don't rush. Your waist will shrink and your food bills will shrink with it. Treat yourself to a concert, a movie, whatever you like. Which of course is the time to point out that eating a small amount of popcorn – preferably not the sugared kind – over the course of a movie is just part of the **EATALL™** way.

HOW TO COPE WITH SOCIAL OCCASIONS THE EATALL™ WAY

MEALS

No, you don't actually have to give these up. They're often great social occasions and can still be enjoyed to the full. Just keep on eating at a slow, steady pace. OK, sometimes we forget and eat quickly, and that may happen to you. It doesn't matter. The body doesn't seem to notice once you're established on the **EATALL™** way. At times you'll actually lose more weight by doing this.

Just remember: if you get full don't forget to keep on eating afterwards. Do *not* fall back into the habit of three square meals a day. If you do you can look forward to weight gain. Keep the body ticking over and keep on feeding it small amounts at regular intervals. That way fat won't to accumulate.

Breakfast

You know this is an important meal; you've been told this umpteen times. But is it really? Isn't it just a good time to get the **EATALL™** way off to a good start? It doesn't mean you have to pile into all those wonderful waffles, pancakes, fried bacon slices, fry-ups etc. You don't have to have a croissant or two, or some of those sweet rolls. But do please have something. Start the day off as soon as you can, get the body going so it can keep on working for you for the rest of the day.

Breakfast meetings are a great time to get business done. That also means you simply won't have time to eat too much. But if you're bored, not really part of the conversation or group, go ahead, take your time and eat whatever takes your fancy but in small amounts.

Lunch

Here we are part of the way through the day. That's not exactly half way unless you get up early and go to bed early. It's sometimes only three or four hours into the waking day. You should have had at least three **EATALL™** portions by then, preferably four or five. So, this is a great time just to meet with some friends, talk, catch up. You don't need to focus on eating. Did you know that a new national survey indicates that one-third of adult Americans, or seventy-one million people, are currently on a diet – an increase of thirty-five percent since the year 2000. These people are generally on a low fat, low carbohydrate diet, so they go for just a salad.

Great; that fits perfectly with the **EATALL™** way. Join them, but make your salad last. And be sure you enjoy it. If you don't go for salad choose something else. You need to enjoy the food; that's part of the **EATALL™** way to success.

If you don't particularly care about food, then it doesn't matter so much what you choose. Keep it healthy if you can. You might even go for the cheapest dish on the menu. Oddly, the two often coincide and you can save some cash.

Remember, this is just one, maybe two, of the many **EATALL™** portions you'll eat during the whole day. It doesn't have to be your favorite; you have plenty more choices to come. If you eat more than you think is right for the method, don't worry, just keep on eating for the rest of the day and so ensure your body won't even notice the extra food you had.

Dinner

OK, we've arrived close to the end of the day for many people, but there are still several **EATALL™** portions to go. Don't give up now. If you let yourself go for dinner, so be it, but don't forget about the **EATALL™** portions that are due later. Make sure you eat them even if the portions are really small.

Take your time over the occasion; enjoy the company and the food. This is a great time to slow down. If eating dinner is just not something you like to do, then don't concern yourself. We're simply giving you a few hints on optimal ways to benefit from the **EATALL™** way. It's up to you to decide whether you accept them or prefer to substitute some of your own ways. That's what's so great. However you apply it the **EATALL™** way will still work for you.

BREAKS

There are occasions when you're expected to eat even though it isn't time for a meal. These shouldn't actually cause much of a problem.

Coffee Breaks

These are perfect for the **EATALL™** way. Just remember a quarter of a doughnut can be spread throughout the whole break... or buy the mini sizes offered by many supermarkets.

The Work Place

Many people feel they cannot eat at work. This means they will miss out on several **EATALL™** portions during a working day. That's not good. Try to find ways to eat something, whether it be a so-called healthy food or not. Even eating a few chips is better than missing an **EATALL™** portion.

Eat a couple of chocolates – Hershey's kisses are ideal – when you have no time for anything else. But, if you plan ahead – and that's easy to do these days with online diaries – you can have an assortment of good healthy food around. Whether it be apple slices, a few nuts, whole wheat crackers, a small amount of cheese, slices of meat, bite-sized quiches, smoked fish, caviar even – all these will keep that hunger away, keep your metabolism going and help you lose that weight. Once you've achieved your weight goal that same strategy will help to maintain it in the future. Where you keep the food or how it's stored and sorted is up to you. Under your desk is fine. In a refrigerator is great. Near a microwave or toaster is fine. You can choose what fits with your work environment and with your boss's predilections, you can choose if the food is cold or hot, you can choose the time and the amount. The main point is to keep control of hunger; not artificially, but with food. Your body will do the rest.

If your work environment is more challenging, and you feel you simply cannot eat in the workplace, then keep some handy packages of biscuits, nuts, whatever is in your desk or in your car. Nibble them surreptitiously, or go to the restroom and eat on the way there. Better still, try to get outside for some fresh air. It's crucial to make certain you've eaten before you even go to the office. Be sure to have something in your car or for eating on the train or bus.

If eating isn't possible, what about drinks? It's quite acceptable for people to go round with a bottle of water from which they drink frequently. Remember that you can drink your food – put some diluted juice in a bottle of water, find an opaque one and substitute tomato or vegetable juice, or use cream in your coffee. All these drinks can be used for an **EATALL™** bite.

You could have a small smoothie, or even an ice cream float. OK, that last idea could be hard to get away with at work, but your boss cannot stop you from drinking, surely.

Business Meetings

These can go on for hours, but there's usually some time allowed for a break. By keeping food in your purse or you briefcase, or even in a backpack, you can make sure you don't get hungry. You can still attend the important meals that are so much a part of negotiations at business meals, just try to follow the **EATALL™** guidelines outlined above.

The great thing about business meetings is that you can take a break every so often. Whether it's to go to the restroom, to chat secretly with your 'team' or, now you're an **EATALL™** person, to have a few private (or even shared) minutes for an **EATALL™** portion. The organizers of scheduled business meetings generally provide snacks such as cookies, muffins or biscuits, which means they are actually sanctioning the **EATALL™** method and you should certainly take advantage.

SOCIAL FUNCTIONS

These events can be difficult to deal with unless you have thought them through beforehand. We include a few suggestions for those you might go to quite frequently.

Galas

These can be fun. All those silent and live auctions are entertaining, providing you have the money to compete. Little snack foods are often passed around, providing a veritable haven for **EATALL™** way partakers. Now you can enjoy those tasty snacks with no guilt feelings.

Remember what we said before, your mother telling you not to snack between meals or you'll ruin your appetite? Well, here's to your mother; she was right on the ball all along. That's what's so great. Go ahead. Enjoy a couple of snacks or more, depending on how long you'll be there. If you're doing well on the **EATALL™** way you'll have been eating all day anyway, so you're probably not hungry. Use the opportunity to have tiny morsels of great food for free, and please go ahead and ruin your appetite.

We love those appetizers. They're usually much better than the main courses on offer. They're served in small sizes and you can choose from a variety of tastes, textures and looks. So don't give up on them. Many dieters avoid them and eat just a main course. We're saying it's better to have two appetizers and no main course. The variety of tastes is greater and thus more satisfying. The amount of Calories may be the same, but they're consumed over a time. If you eat just a small portion of each one then the Calorie intake will be reduced and the resulting weight loss will be achieved more quickly.

When it comes time to have the main meal and you've eaten the **EATALL™** way all day, you won't be that hungry. You can enjoy a

59

small portion of whatever is placed in front of you. The thing with Galas is that there'll be a speaker talking while you eat. Interesting or boring as the speaker may be, you can now take plenty of time over eating whatever they put in front of you. And the best thing is you didn't even have to cook it – and it will probably taste great. If not, then what do you care if you simply leave it on the plate and move onto the next, hopefully better, course? Alternatively just leave, as so many other bored people do. Go to the car for some food that you keep there and will actually like.

Charity Events

Like Galas, these can be great for those eating the **EATALL™** way. You might feel guilty about leaving food on your plate. Just forget it, or find someone at your table who needs – or wants – that food. There's usually someone who'll be keen to eat your share. And there are always teenagers who'll help out with dessert.

Depending on the style of the event, the food available may be awful. Simply eat what you can to keep your body going. If, on the other hand, it's great stuff, then wonderful, go for it and take small portions of whatever is good.

Formal Dinners

Wonderful snacks are often served before the meal itself. Enjoy nibbling on them – they're perfect for the **EATALL™** way. The rest of a formal dinner may be harder to bend to the **EATALL™** way than **Galas** or **Charity Events**. In some ways formal dinners are quite difficult to handle diplomatically. The problem is that someone has paid a fortune for this meal, so the pressure to eat all the food on the plate will be substantial. Just remember that even if you feel obliged to eat more than you want to, it's not the end of the world. The main thing is not to feel guilty.

Surprisingly, the occasional large meal, as discussed above, can be a blessing in disguise. You'll lose more weight because the body is taken by surprise. You *can* eat meals – just follow our message.

HOW TO DEAL WITH FESTIVITIES

Festivities are the hardest times of year for many people. It's after these occasions that people decide they must diet. Not for anyone eating the **EATALL™** way. All it takes is to remember to consume **EATALL™** portions and to keep to **EATALL™** times, and there won't be any need to worry.

Yes, you *can* indulge in large portions. You probably won't want to, but if you do, no worries. And, just because you pile your plate high because that's what you've always done, doesn't mean you have to eat it all. The point is you can still have all the tastes of the food you desire (whether you need it or not) and your body will adapt. It can even be a great time to start practicing the **EATALL™** way, as there are so many foods to choose from and people tend to be more relaxed and have time to spend over the meals.

What is even better is that festivities lead to leftovers – lots of leftovers. How ideal an environment that is for the **EATALL™** way. You won't eat that much at meals compared to your colleagues (unless, like you, they're using the **EATALL™** way) but they will be envious that you get to eat all the rest of the day without any guilt feelings. You won't feel uncomfortably full, you'll have had the enjoyment of festive food, and you'll be very happy.

If you're the cook you'll probably have done a great deal of tasting already; that's an excellent way to get your **EATALL™** portions, just remember that you have had some.

Thanksgiving

This is a great time for lean, healthy meat – turkey is one of the best around. Have a small piece or even two. Or eat it every hour. It's your choice. Have a small portion of potato or yam or sweet potato – or eat it all day long. Remember that both apple and cranberry sauces may contain a lot of sugar, so eat them slowly and sparingly, but your reward is that you can eat them all day long. The pies – oh those pies! From a Calorie point of view the worst is pecan and the least damaging is pumpkin. Taste them all, just make sure you do so in small amounts.

Remember, you're not trying to get full; you're not in a rush. Eat for the taste and then do something else. Play games with the kids, talk with whoever will share time with you. Then go back and eat a little more. Spread those great tastes over time and you'll eat less than the others around you, enjoy the taste far more, make the others envious, and above all lose weight or maintain your lovely figure.

Christmas and Chanukah

If in doubt celebrate both. The more presents to give or be given the better, right? But do remember that those wonderful plum pies eaten with brandy butter are bursting with Calories. However, they can be enjoyed over time and in small amounts. Ham – not as healthy as turkey and certainly not Kosher – can also be eaten in small slices and over time.

The potato latkes with apple sauce are wonderful. You have so many days to eat them, so that's the way to go. Have a small one each day, don't eat them all when they're first served. Both latkes and apple sauce are full of Calories. Remember you don't have to eat large amounts, the taste is all you need. The more frequently you eat them the more you'll enjoy them compared to eating them all at once the first night. Take your time, play the Dreidle. Win some money or boost your ego and then go back for more small portions.

Easter and Passover

There are so many holidays – almost one a month, so don't let us limit you. Celebrate them all without a care. You'll be able to enjoy them without the guilt that others suffer. You can even use them to lose weight.

Those Easter eggs are wonderful. Eat a couple of the tiny ones, but go for quality if you have a choice, and enjoy. Wait for more **EATALL™** times to pass and repeat. Treat the Easter cake in the same way.

Passover is a little different, but the great thing is that the meal is meant to last quite a while. Take your time, read the story and enjoy the foods – one at a time as they come to be discussed. When you finally get to the main course you won't be hungry. You'll be able to munch on small **EATALL™** portions.

Cocktail Parties

There is no problem about following the **EATALL™** way when attending a cocktail party. No one is going to notice how many of those delightful **EATALL™** way portions you eat, but of course it is up to you not to eat more than a couple every forty-five to sixty minutes.

Choosing what you are going to drink part may take a little more thought. Try to choose a long drink that you really like; it's easier to practice your sipping powers. Why not go for that a glass of champagne? It's easy to make that last for at least an hour.

It's very easy to swallow several **EATALL™** portions before you realize what's happening. Educate yourself before you go to that party. Here's a simple, down-to-earth site:

http://www.at-bristol.org.uk/Alcoholandyou/Facts/calories.html

Wedding Receptions

This depends, of course, on whether the wedding is a formal, sit-down affair or similar to a cocktail party. For the latter, see above. For a formal meal where you are often sitting with friends and relatives who might be upset if you leave all the food they have so carefully planned and paid for, you may have to eat more than your usual amount. Eat slowly; put your cutlery back on the plate between mouthfuls. Eventually a waiter will come and ask if you've finished

Celebrations marking Religious Occasions

You know the sort of occasion we mean: Baptisms, Bar and Bat Mitzvahs, First Communions, any occasion on which people get together to celebrate with their families and friends. Just follow the suggestions for Cocktail Parties and Wedding Receptions.

My Birthday

Celebrate! It only comes once a year and, like all the other special holidays, you can easily make it adapt to the **EATALL™** way.

MISCELLANEOUS QUESTIONS

One of the big stumbling blocks for dieting are the times we eat with other people. A really big plus point for the **EATALL™** method of losing and keeping off weight is that you can 'cheat' a little without feeling you have to start over. You just carry on eating. Now isn't that quite something?

What do I do at family mealtimes?

Well, you can act just like you always did and simply gorge yourself.

Better not. Try to change the way you take in food over the day. By the time the meal arrives try not to be hungry. Be sure not to save yourself up for the meal. That way you won't eat any more than you want or should. But, if you *are* hungry, then try to take small portions, spread them out to look larger, move the food around on your plate, just like you did as a kid when you didn't want to eat, remember? Eat slowly, chewing each mouthful as much as you can. And if your plate is heaped by someone else, leave some food, or get someone else to eat it. Whatever you do won't affect the starving millions in Africa – eat it or waste it, they don't get it. Right?

If you feel guilty here's a really good opportunity to donate the money you'll save by eating the **EATALL™** way; you might even be able to double the amount you usually give to your favorite charity.

Can I drink with my EATALL™ portions?

No problem. In fact it will help you make the food go further, and you can spend time sipping instead of eating. Just remember that anything apart from water is a food – in liquid form. And there is no problem about including wine; in fact red wine is said to be helpful as a preventative for heart disease. So include wine if you enjoy it. We say more about this topic later.

What if I feel really hungry?

First, drink some water. Then, eat something slowly, until you no longer feel hungry. Your body does have its own, built-in cut-off point, but you have to give it time to become aware of it. So, slowly does it. If you feel you just have to eat a lot, then go ahead. Just keep on eating **EATALL™** portions afterwards so the hunger will not return. This happens to us all – we simply forget – but you can readily get right back on track with no harm done.

What about meat?

Some people think that meat is full of Calories. It's a dense food but, as with fruit and other sugar-laden foods, don't deprive yourself of meat because it's high on Calories. Of course you won't have this problem if you're a vegetarian.

Calories are important, but they don't count as much as eating the **EATALL™** way. Keep Calories down as much as you can, as that can only help, but you certainly need them – it's just a matter of choosing, very approximately, how many and when.

So, go ahead and eat meat. If you have a choice you might like to go for the less Calorie-laden meats, such as turkey or chicken breast. Even have a thick steak every now and again if that is what you really want. Try to remember not to do it too often and do your best to keep the portion size down. Thoroughly chew each mouthful of meat, try to eat slowly by pausing between bites. Go for lean meat if you have a choice, and remember that you just need enough to keep from being hungry. If you practice the **EATALL™** way you'll find that you don't even want that big steak, or won't be able to eat it all. Instead you'll keep some for the next **EATALL™** portion.

What if I forget to eat?

Just start again as soon as you remember. It will take a little time for you to get into the right habit, but you'll get there. You could invest in one of those watches which can be set to chime or buzz each hour or whatever.

If you're letting hunger be your clock you're not using the **EATALL™** way, you're using the gorging method of eating. Some people have a hard time getting used to the method. That's fine, just use other ways to remind yourself. And, if eating between meals goes against the ingrained, don't eat very much. Nibble, but try to do it at least every hour. Try hard to ruin your appetite.

What if I have a health problem?

If you're on a restricted diet because of a health problem, stick to that diet but ask your doctor if you can cut the portions down and eat every hour or less.

Your doctor may not see the point of the **EATALL™** way to begin with, but it shouldn't take too long to show that what you're doing isn't harmful in any way. See if your doctor can make his prescribed diet fit within the **EATALL™** way.

What about chocolate?

You can eat chocolate – preferably, like everything else, in small amounts. Bar chocolate is usually marked into individual portions. Break each bar into its sections and only keep one or two within easy reach. Each section will probably make up one **EATALL™** portion, but you can probably enjoy two without any problems.

Good quality, dark chocolate is now even being touted as a health food in small amounts – just like a glass of red wine. And did you know that the proper way to get the most from your chocolate is to let it melt – slowly – on your tongue? It's the best way to savor that blissful taste, and it fits beautifully into the **EATALL™** way. Just so you know the authors of this book are both chocoholics, so it had better be part of the **EATALL™** way for us.

What if I can't manage without candies?

Eat them. But, as with chocolate, preferable don't chew them – suck them, and get the most enjoyment out of them. As above, have your sugar in a form that you really enjoy and not in indifferent food, like sliced white bread. Have a candy instead of that bread. Just keep the total Calories down. If it's whole wheat bread with low sugar – hey, no worries. Be aware that white bread made with refined flour is almost as bad as a candy. As mentioned before, the Calories do count, so they're important, but not as important as the timing.

If you keep hunger away you'll eat less automatically. If you find you're eating just for something to do, then eat food without many Calories, like celery sticks. Eating candies under those circumstances will certainly not help you lose weight.

As an example, if you're served a sandwich – eat the meat and the cheese and the vegetables inside the sandwich and leave the bread. Do that, then later on you can 'afford' to eat that candy you so want. One sacrifice at one **EATALL™** time can be rewarded – as soon as the next **EATALL™** time comes around.

What if my friends want to go out for a celebration meal?

Join them, but order appetizers instead of the main course. Make it last. It can take an hour to eat a salad if you want it to. Are you going for the food, or for the company? Exactly.

If one of your friends has joined you in the **EATALL™** way, share your food. Until, that is, the day restaurants catch on to serving **EATALL™** portions. Sharing is a great way to have more tastes to enjoy. Eating the **EATALL™** way ensures you're more interested in taste and feel than in actually getting full. Others eat at meals to get full so they don't get hungry later. They're trying to keep themselves satisfied for at least a few hours. You, on the other hand, are just eating for the joy of the taste and to keep hunger away until the next **EATALL™** portion time.

I love junk food

That isn't so good for you. But you can eat whatever you like using the **EATALL™** way. Buy some junk food but order a small size. Make it last, share it with a friend. By the time you're through you'll long for a good salad or some nice fresh fruit. It's the gobbling which hides how disgusting some of that food really is.

This isn't meant to give you license to eat tons of junk food, it's just being realistic. You'll get the desire, so just go for it and fill that craving. Try to do it the **EATALL™** way. Ultimately you'll learn not to have such desires, or that when they're fulfilled it wasn't worth it – but that can take years. So, for now, at least eat the **EATALL™** way.

I feel dizzy

You may not be eating enough. Just drink some water, eat a piece of candy (for rapid energy) or any other food if you feel faint. You'll get used to what your body needs pretty quickly.

Should I take supplements?

That decision has nothing to do with the method. If you take them now, carry on. If not, and you think you're not getting all the vitamins and minerals you need, take a good multivitamin. These shouldn't hurt you, but that doesn't make it a recommendation. Some of the companies that sell some of these supplements are not what you would call driven to assist your health as opposed to their own financial health – so just use your best judgment.

I want the main course

Have it, as discussed above. Just try not to eat all of it. Find someone to share it, or someone who'll be happy to take some of it from you. Or take the leftovers home in a doggy bag to enjoy later.

I can't get away every hour

Slip a piece of chocolate into your mouth when no one's looking. Anyway, what if they do see? Or add tomato juice or fruit juice to your water bottle. No one seems to worry about people drinking all the time.

What about flying?

You can buy snacks once you're through security. You can drink juices. The airlines offer tomato juice which is an OK food disguised as a drink – just be aware of all the sugar added to that juice by some manufacturers. There are many ways to make the **EATALL™** way work for you for every occasion. It's easy to carry crackers in a clear plastic bag or handbag. Some airlines sell food on the plane. It may not be that healthy, but it will be adequate for some **EATALL™** portions.

What if I'm in hospital?

Ask your visitors to bring you your favorite foods. Check with your doctor to make sure there are no medical issues. For example, you certainly cannot eat for many hours before an operation. So plan ahead, and just get back on track after the operation.

What if I'm on a catered holiday?

Eat the **EATALL™** way, get some extras for between their meals. Some holidays are just made for the **EATALL™** way. On cruises, for example, there are always plenty of snacks around . They provide a perfect system for having varied and even healthy **EATALL™** portions just when you want or need them.

You can drink

The food you put into your body isn't just solids, of course. A large part of what you ingest is in liquid form. Just remember that alcohol is relatively high in Calories and requires very little digesting.

Liquid food

What concerns us for the **EATALL™** way is that some liquids are actually foods. Milk, for example. So if you want to keep to the **EATALL™** principles a whole glass of milk would count as one **EATALL™** portion. The same goes for a cup of hot chocolate, or coffee with cream, or wine, or beer, or any liquid which has an appreciable Calorie count. The fact that it's in liquid form doesn't actually affect its status as a food.

There is one way in which liquids are easier to deal with than solid food. The glass or cup size determines the amount you drink neatly and accurately. If you enjoy drinking milk, or drinks made with milk, you already know to use non-fat milk for a lower Calorie count. You can also put your drink into a small glass rather than a tumbler, and sip, or use a narrow straw if you like. It's amazing how quickly one becomes adept at that sort of stratagem.

You've probably read that caffeine affects weight loss, and should be cut out. We have no definite opinions on that, but both of us gave up caffeine years ago without any affect one way or the other. It's a choice for you, or between you and your doctor. In fact another BBC study shows that, though caffeine has an initial stimulating effect, not drinking caffeine in no way decreases a person's alertness – well, not after the initial cold turkey period, anyway.

Fruit juices

Remember that fruit juices are not exactly Calorie free. A small glass of orange juice may be made from four or five oranges, and will contain around 150 Calories – more than a gin with diet tonic. Watermelon juice has a few less Calories, but it's almost pure sugar, as is pineapple juice which is also heavier on the Calories. Tomato and vegetable juices may be good for you, but they, too, are calorific. To get over this problem use a small amount of your favorite juice, add sparkling water or ice and water, sip. You get the benefit of the taste of the juice, you get a reasonable amount of liquid and you don't use up a large **EATALL™** portion.

Water

As no doubt you already know, many diets advocate drinking water; not just while you're dieting, but all the time. The usual injunction is to drink eight glasses of water a day, in addition to your normal consumption of tea, coffee, sodas and whatever else you drink. The rationale for this is that water flushes out impurities.

The body needs liquid and especially water as much as it needs food. You cannot live long without water, though you can survive as much as three weeks without food.

Some people think drinking eight glasses of water a day is too much unless you live in a very dry climate – like San Diego, for example. If you drink several cups of tea or coffee without milk, and some watered-down fruit juices and diet sodas, then fewer glasses of water might be enough. But that's for you and your body to decide.

In a recent BBC program – *The Truth about Food* – a pair of twins was asked to take liquid in two ways: one twin faithfully drank the eight glasses of water on top of her usual intake of food and drink, the other just drank what people normally drink with their food.

The result? Not a scrap of difference between the two systems. The body got plenty of liquid from the normal diet, and simply excreted the excess on the other diet. Flushing the kidneys? Apparently extra water doesn't have that effect.

Alcohol

Avoiding alcohol will help you lose weight – if you drank it before trying to slim, that is. If that isn't a price you're willing to pay, then follow the **EATALL™** way and use the alcohol you drink as one **EATALL™** portion. Combine it with a high-bulk, low Calorie solid like celery or pickles to give you a feeling of satiety. That way you can have your drink and eat it, too.

Drinking wine can be turned into a connoisseur affair. Take a tip from wine lovers – only fill your glass one quarter to one third full, twirl the wine around to aerate it and sniff the bouquet. Then sip it, don't swallow it all in one go. The whole procedure takes time and looks very professional and impressive. Instead of swigging cheap wine why not buy expensive wine and savor it, sip by sip? You'll actually save money, and enjoy it far more.

For spirits you can order or make a small cocktail rather than a large one. You can always make another one later for one more **EATALL™** portion. Better still; add a diet chaser, or lots of ice. Maybe you can drink spirits with a mixer – whisky and water or diet soda, rum and diet coke. What we're saying is that you can still have drinks if you had them before you started on the **EATALL™** way. Just use them sparingly, and enjoy them over a longer period of time.

Appreciate them like an **EATALL™** portion of solid food.

So, if you enjoyed drinking wine with your meals, or to have a drink with your friends, before you started on the **EATALL™** way, you'll certainly lose weight just by avoiding alcohol. We're saying that if having a drink is something you relish don't cut it out; instead, treat each drink as an **EATALL™** portion. It may be high in Calories, especially when topped by liqueurs which ooze sugar, but the feeling of enjoyment will almost certainly be worth the Calorie price. Enjoy your food and drink; that's what will make the **EATALL™** way work for you. Incidentally, liqueurs are very useful when making desserts, because a tiny amount will create a great taste.

Water again

The most important liquid of all is water. You can buy bottled water at any supermarket, and the choice is extensive. But why not invest in a water filter? It gets rid of a great many contaminants, makes the water taste better, brews fresh-tasting tea, herb tea and coffee, makes flavorful soups and is available straight from the tap. Silver tea – hot water drunk like tea – is great in cold weather. Learn to love water as a drink. You may, eventually, find you prefer it to most others. And there's nothing better for quenching thirst.

If you want to go in for gourmet waters, by all means do. They're fairly costly, but if you wish to substitute them for sodas or fruit juices, it might be worth it. As mentioned above you can flavor them with small amounts of your favorite juice. Sparkling water added to fruit juices can make a significant difference to lowering the number of Calories taken in, yet still give you the taste you love.

Water has one other quality which makes it really valuable. It can make your stomach feel full. So, if you do get hunger pangs, try drinking a glass of water, then eating your **EATALL™** portion. If you're worried that the water will dilute your digestive juices add a teaspoon of cider vinegar to the glass of water. This vinegar has the most remarkable properties. Sip a glass spiced with one teaspoon when you feel queasy and it will make you feel better in no time. It's also said to help you slim, clear your arteries, help with arthritic joints, and to cure mastitis. It may just be folk medicine, but some of it seems to work.

To Exercise, or not to exercise?

Richard's thoughts

I love exercise, I can watch it all day is a witticism you've probably come across before. Coming from the UK originally I wasn't really brought up with the idea that one must exercise all the time. Don't get me wrong, I love to play games, all kinds of games. I've even came up with a board game that is now sold world wide. But I don't see the point of merely running around a track, or on a road and especially on a machine that seems never to go anywhere. I need to be distracted to actually exercise, so in reality it wasn't something up there in my priorities.

That has changed in the last few years. I found out how to con myself into burning some Calories – whether playing badminton, or watching a movie while on an elliptical machine. We all know that exercise is likely to help control one's figure and one's weight. Few of us really enjoy this fact and even fewer follow through. So, I won't bother to lecture you. Go read another book for that. But, if you can find a way that you enjoy while burning a few Calories then you're on the path to a great way to get your exercise.

There are so many subtle ways to do this. It's purely psychological for the majority of us. Or, we simply don't have the time, or more likely (admit it) don't make the time. We're not all compulsive enough to get up at four in the morning and go running – at least not more than once a year when we're really feeling guilty or motivated.

Think about it, though. Do you like to dance, walk, paint, fish, garden? Add whatever exercise you enjoy to that activity and so find a way to burn a few more Calories. Dancing and walking are easy, simply find a partner and go for it. Or join a group to make it more interesting. Walk to a better spot for painting or fishing.

Think about the kind of exercise you can do which will not only burn Calories but achieve something else as well. Clean your own house, decorate it, mow your own lawn. Take the kids or grandkids to the park or beach. Join them in their games. You don't have to win or be good at whatever they play – leave that to them.

Every little helps. Even if not that many Calories are burned, psychologically you've achieved a great deal. And even walking a couple of blocks more every day will increase your metabolism. Take it one step at a time.

I used to think it great if I exercised ten minutes a day, now I can do four or more times that amount. It takes time to get used to it – but the time to start is now. Your choice, of course. Remember, the more variety the better as you're more likely to keep going.

I'm sure you know that even walking burns lots of Calories and gets your muscles going. You don't have to run; in many ways it's better for your weight-bearing joints not to, anyway.

If you choose weird times of the day to perform these activities it will make it harder for you – just make sure this isn't a fad and you'll actually be able to keep going. Don't set a goal you can't achieve. Set small-step goals and reward yourself.

Bottom line: doing a reasonable amount of exercise cannot be bad; just do it consistently. Remember a few minutes here and there can be as good as a solid time all at once. Make it easy on yourself. Lifting weights helps but is very boring. Reorganize your room instead. Move heavy books around on your shelves, change the furniture, have fun.

Enough already, you say. I agree, I am done – good luck.

PSYCHOLOGY AND THE EATALL™ WAY

Why does this way work for many people where other methods fail? Diets are tough to stick to. You follow them to the letter (yeah, right) and they work for a short time. You lose some weight, pat yourself on the back – and go back to old habits.

Of course this doesn't just apply to you. Celebrities have just as hard a time, and for many of them their careers depend on a slim figure. Also, most of them have the advantage of personal trainers or even personal chefs. As soon as they're on their own they fail again. No need to mention names, but it's amazing how people simply cannot stick to diets and have to go on a binge to get over them.

A lady at a party the other day was clearly overweight. She explained that she was just too busy with work and so never exercised. She had more excuses than extra pounds. But the bottom line was she'd given up trying to control her weight. She liked to eat and, for her, that was more important than staying trim. When told about the **EATALL™** way she was excited, and no wonder. The **EATALL™** way is a method that works brilliantly if you change just one thing: eat small amounts at frequent intervals instead of large amounts two or three times a day. Once your body has adjusted you can even eat your meals again – the secret is to just keep eating.

The biggest problem for most people is that they like to eat. They get hungry – well 'duh'. The question is, how do we stop that hunger, both physically and the psychologically? Do we fill people up with chemicals to block their stomachs? Do we advise food that has no taste and no Calories or, as a last resort, do we even cut the stomach, then stitch it together, in a poor replica of the organ it used to be?

Not if you use the **EATALL™** way . We advise eating reasonable amounts of food on a fairly continuous basis, giving the feeling of a plentiful food supply and never allowing hunger to appear.

Perceived hunger

Just what is hunger? It's the body telling you it needs food, or it's the mind seeing food and saying: 'Cool, let's eat.' Therefore if you simply have food available but not too visible you can munch on that food regularly but not get distracted by it. It becomes part of your lifestyle. You can still have meals – and you'll probably eat less at those meals – but your body will still burn the food up and not store fat.

Now, as we've emphasized before, we're not advocating that you eat huge meals and have huge amounts of food between those meals. Absolutely not; everything has to be within reason. And we do admit this system won't work for some people. They say they don't have time, or opportunity, to eat all the time.

In reality it takes very little time. If you have the food around, you can eat it in less than a minute. No, we're not saying that is optimal, but it's better than not doing so. After just a couple days you won't feel any hunger at all, and you won't care about the meals. You'll be losing pounds. Even better, with a little luck, you'll be *waisting* away.

But, you may object, I must have meals for my business, for my significant other, for my kids. No worries; go right ahead. The difference is you'll be using that meal as one or two of your **EATALL™** times. You can eat all the food if you want. The point is you just won't want to. Even if you see food and want to eat it the urge won't be as great, and won't last as long. You'll see food and be happy to leave it.

If everyone else is rushing through the meal just eat a little and be done like they are. If they're taking their time, then so can you.

Maybe you like to gulp your food down, you just don't like eating slowly. Well, so do we, believe it or not. But if you focus you can stop yourself. First of all you aren't even hungry. That means you'll take smaller portions. You won't have the urge to gobble food to get through it all. Instead you'll find yourself picking at it.

For example, Richard was in a bar one night (no, this is not a bar joke) after having been on an airplane all day, returning from a business trip. He'd been eating crackers and airplane food. That alone can help you lose weight. He really wasn't that hungry but knew that he should have an **EATALL™** portion as it was too early to go to bed. He had a drink and a salad. It took about an hour to eat just half the salad – and he was full. So, just trust yourself and your body. The first few days may be quite challenging – or, if you're lucky, maybe not. After that it simply becomes routine.

PSYCHOLOGICAL BARRIERS

Comfort eating

There are a couple of psychological barriers which may cause problems to start with. Most of us, in our childhood, were given food – usually chocolate or candy – as a reward, or to make us feel better after a minor fall, or as a special treat. It set up our minds to equate food, particularly certain types of food, with feeling good. So when, in adult life, there is a crisis, we often turn to food to make us feel better. Sometimes this extends to a need to a feeling for fullness, even of bloating, in the stomach, or perhaps a need to have something constantly in one's mouth.

Fortunately the **EATALL™** way allows us to fulfill most of those needs without putting on pounds. And, after a time, the need seems to fall away. We who live in the developed world know that food will always be available; we don't need to do anything special to deserve it. And we can send the money we save to all those millions who have a different diet problem from ours: they can't get enough food.

Greed

Another little problem, to put it bluntly, is greed. You go to a social function, delightful canapés are spread out for your delight, you take a plate – and heap it. It's natural to want to taste everything, the food's so tempting. And if you don't heap your plate right then and there you may not get a second chance. Well, that's the answer. Take a small amount – you don't *want* that second chance. Be greedy about the pounds you'll lose.

Envy

Yet another psychological barrier is envy. Why should all these other people be able to indulge in their favorite foods while you have to stand (or sit) there nibbling at bird food? They heap their plates, they fill their glasses and they even raise them to you in a toast - while you sip your water.

That can be tough. Now look at their waistlines. OK, some of them are young and can get away with it. But not for long. And, very soon, you'll be the one they'll envy.

Fear

One thing that may be putting you off trying this approach is fear of failure. This fear, coming from trying several diets with which you succeeded at first, then found yourself slipping back into weight gain – possibly a greater gain than before you went on the diet – is very real.

We feel that the **EATALL™** way won't let you down because there isn't anything you *can't* eat. And that makes all the difference. Whatever you do, you can get back to eating small portions, even if you've just indulged in a mammoth meal.

Satisfaction

The **EATALL™** way works because it's easy to remember to eat; you get to eat whatever you really like and you do it all the time. We're not telling you to diet, we're not forbidding any foods. You already know what you should eat – you've read all the books, or listened to the advertising on TV – but people always ignore what is known to be good for them. You'll cheat, of course. We all do, all the time, but the **EATALL™** way will still work as the body will keep on chugging away. That is why, if you adopt this method, you'll have a really great chance to succeed. And, as the rest of the world starts to understand and embrace the **EATALL™** way, it can only become easier.

Living the Method

Timing is not so critical once you're using the **EATALL™** way. The first two days are the most important. But that's just the beginning. After a while you can adjust the time to suit yourself. You can eat every fifteen minutes, or every two hours. It all depends on your particular body.

There is one other fact that may make it easier for you to change to this new way of eating. It's been known since the Thirties that you will almost certainly live longer if you eat less. Another little encouragement is that your food bills will be lower, and that, at a time of global warming and increasing world populations, may become a factor even in the affluent developed world.

It's well-known that women find it harder to slim than men. Unfair? Maybe; but statistically they live longer, therefore on average they have seven extra years in which to eat. So what's fair about that?

Those who are nearly slim already, or those who are overweight or even obese, will find that the body tells them what's going to work for them. Listen to your body. Eat until you no longer feel hungry.

What was that? What we mean is not to eat a meal so that you get full, and then wait for the next meal. That's the old, proven way to gain weight. What we suggest is that you eat a little, wait half an hour or an hour, then eat again. See what you need to eat so that the next **EATALL™** time doesn't seem too long away. Vary the period with your mood, your feelings, your schedule – whatever. But try to maintain a level of food in your body that is sufficient to stop you from being hungry, but not so great that you're stuffing yourself.

That's the key.

You want to make it so you're comfortable with eating or not eating, it shouldn't matter. Now, this isn't nearly as difficult as it sounds and we'll give you several hints later on.

ACHIEVING WEIGHT LOSS TARGETS

Everyone seems to be focused on Calories these days. And there is good reason for that. But we recognize that all Calories are *not* created equal. For example, you can have as many as you like in protein form – the body simply excretes those you don't need. But, since everyone thinks in terms of Calories, we provide a rough guide in that language here. The bottom line for us, however, is to:

> ***Eat an average of about one fifteenth of the total food that you need in any one day on every hour.***

Total caloric requirements for each day

The daily caloric requirement for the average woman with a sedentary lifestyle is roughly 1700 Calories, while that of the average man is roughly 2500 Calories. For a moderately active lifestyle the average woman would need perhaps 2100 Calories, the average man 2800.

These numbers are based on average heights, and are simply guidelines; individuals vary substantially in their needs. You can get precise numbers from formulae available on the web – we don't need to repeat them here. See, for example:

http://www.freedieting.com/tools/calorie_calculator.htm.

Just enter your particulars and you'll easily be able to find the magic number. Please remember that sites move, disappear and change their names. You can always find more by searching in Google or other search engines.

To find out how much you need for each **EATALL™** portion total the Calories you eat on an average day, or use the results from the above website. For your normal requirement divide this personal amount by seventeen to arrive at an approximation of the Calories needed for each **EATALL™** portion.

That works out at around 120 Calories for each **EATALL™** portion for the average woman and roughly 150 Calories for the average man, assuming a sedentary lifestyle for both. Or, if you only want to eat fifteen times a day, the figures would be 130 and 170.

Do remember that these are average figures; you need to research what is needed for your particular gender, age, lifestyle and the amount you weigh at the moment.

If you're within 10lb (5kg) of your ideal weight

If you're already reasonably slender, say weighing in the 100-130 lb (45.5–9.5 kg) for a 5 ft 3 in (1.60m) woman or 145–165 lb (66–75 kg) for a 5 ft 9 in (1.75m) man, and want to lose those last few pounds or go down a dress, pants or shirt size and keep it that way, eat just 100 Calories or even less for each **EATALL™** portion. A small woman might want to consider 80 Calorie portions.

We suggest a lot of choices later in the book; you might consider tomatoes combined with some cheese, or perhaps a few crackers. Whatever you choose, it's important to eat an equivalent number of Calories in the foods of your choice at least every hour. That will be a good approximation to what you need to eat to lose some weight. Vary the content, change the timing to every thirty to ninety minutes. That way you won't get bored or suffer from malnutrition.

If you're slightly overweight

If you're a little overweight, say in the 130-160 lb (59.5-72 kg) for a 5 ft 3 in (1.60m) woman or 165-195 lb (75-87.5 kg) for a 5 ft 9 in (1.75m) man, that same method should work, but you can have more in each portion. Increase it by 50% perhaps if you need to keep hunger at bay. Gradually cut down on the amount as you lose weight.

If you're even heavier, or significantly overweight, either of the above will work. It really depends on what your body is used to. If you eat a lot, then the portions will probably have to be larger to start with, and get smaller as you lose weight and your body gets used to taking in less food at a time.

If you already don't eat that much, then keep the portions as above. The idea is that if you have a stable weight you try to eat what you already eat or a bit less, but *eat more frequently*. It's been shown to be healthier. As you get used to the process you should reduce the portion size and even increase the frequency of eating to achieve reasonably rapid weight loss.

The choices are up to you – do whatever you find will work for you bearing in mind your habits, your work, your friends and, above all, your particular body.

Heavier People

What if you weigh over 250 lb and you're a strong, solid man? Then go ahead, you may need a lot of food, perhaps around 3500 Calories each day, especially if you work out. That means your **EATALL™** portions will be double those of people who are within a few pounds of their ideal weight.

Start off with larger portions; reduce them as the method starts to help you to rid yourself of hunger pangs. Your body will help you understand what is needed and what is just simply not needed. It's important that you learn to listen to it.

At first you may not hear what it has to say; well, in that case, just ensure that your body listens to you. Believe us: as you get used to the **EATALL™** way you'll be very comfortable with what you can eat, and what you can no longer stand to even look at, let alone contemplate putting inside your body.

Timing

The timing is, to some extent, critical: the more often you can eat the better, but many people simply cannot seem to make that work. In that case either try to accommodate the process or make the best of it you can. Even eating every two hours is better than the three meals a day regime. If you decide to choose the two hour option it means, unfortunately, that you'll need to eat more at those times and have to be more stringent as to the types of food you eat.

We really believe that most of us can take a break from what we're doing every forty-five to ninety minutes, and spend a couple of minutes (longer if you can) having an **EATALL™** portion of food. It is, in any case, hard to concentrate for longer periods of time, and the brief break away from whatever you're doing will have great benefits for resetting your brain and allowing it to be more productive. That's quote a bonus for a method that you're adopting just to take off weight.

Traveling

Those of us who have to travel long distances will have no problem applying the **EATALL™** way. You can simply provide yourself with a collection of easy-to-open packages in the car, train, plane, boat or bus, or take along a number of re-sealable containers containing mouthwatering food you've prepared for yourself. Don't be embarrassed to eat. Remember people drink all the time and that is perfectly acceptable – indeed, in desert climates, you'd be foolish not to do so. So why should it be a problem to have something to eat?

We aren't limiting what you choose to eat, so don't fuss the details, just eat what you like – but remember that it's only sensible to make sure you choose at least some healthy foods. You know the drill: eat some protein, some complex carbs, some vegetables etc. But with the **EATALL™** way you can also have some Hershey's kisses, small chocolates and even cake when there's nothing else – or have it simply because you like that kind of food. Just try not to eat that all the time. You're free, of course, to make healthier choices. The **EATALL™** way is not stopping you – in fact it encourages that. Just don't let the choices get in the way of your goal of losing weight.

One of the difficulties for people trying the **EATALL™** way for the first time is that there are too many choices. We're not telling you what to do. That's the reason it will work in the long term. We're not telling you what you can no longer eat, or what you must eat. We're just telling you to eat!

For those who like suggested choices, we have included ideas. These cover the size of the **EATALL™** portions, the type of food, useful ways of preparing it and indications of what works best for different people: men and women, kids, teenagers, adults young and old. They all have different requirements, and most of us already know very well what those are.

Shopping the EATALL™ way

Some of the larger discount stores sell excellent, cheap food but they tend to sell it in huge amounts. They won't let you buy a pound of apples — they only sell them in ten pound bags. You can't buy a doughnut, or even six. Instead they come in packaging containing twenty-four large doughnuts. Many of the customers shopping in these stores are also large. After squeezing through the check-out aisles you can see them stuffing themselves with food in the cafeteria. They may be eating a large slice of pizza, or a huge dish of lasagna, or a one-foot hot dog.

How do you deal with a society in which this is the norm? We all know it's part of our fabric, our culture, our freedom to eat as much and how we wish. And that is at it should be.

What, unfortunately, we can guarantee is that most readers of this book will see these people eating, and immediately want some of that food as well. No worries. Once you're eating the **EATALL™** way you simply won't be able to eat food in large quantities. You'll take a few bites, enjoy the taste and, hopefully, throw the rest away before you're tempted to eat it all.

If you do eat it all, so be it, just keep on eating an **EATALL™** portion at the next **EATALL™** time. You may see a bagel stuffed with cream cheese and your mouth will start to water. Go ahead, eat a piece of it. You'll think it huge in just a couple of days, wonder how you ever managed in the past. In fact you'll resist the urge to simply eat it all. You'll take a bite — none of us is exempt from temptation —

and that bite will make you feel full. Then learn to immediately throw away the rest or save it for another **EATALL™** portion later.

Switch to stores selling smaller quantities

It's true that you can save money by buying your food in bulk. But you may not need the large amounts you needed before you learned to eat the **EATALL™** way.

You might like to consider shopping in smaller, more expensive supermarkets or even health food stores. Though the individual foods may be more expensive your total grocery bill may still be lower – because you simply won't need all that food anymore.

As your portions grow smaller you may like to consider buying pricier but healthier food. You may even choose to go organic – and you'll be able to afford to do so. Another choice is to buy only Fair Trade foods. You'll easily be able to afford them, and at the same time you can help food producers in developing countries to earn a decent living. Several advantages with one stone – a stone, by the way, is the old-fashioned UK measure equal to 14 lb.

MODERN MEALTIMES

Traditional family meals served a different purpose in the past. Much work was back-breaking manual labor. Men worked the land, dug in coal mines, labored on building sites, went to sea to fish. These workers needed large, heavy meals to replenish the Calories lost. Cooking such meals, without modern equipment, was a heavy job in itself and kept their wives busy, trim and satisfied with their jobs.

That's an outdated way to eat for the way we live now, but it's traditional, and consequently, for many of us, is considered sacred. That's understandable. Eating three square meals a day worked fine for many generations – until the Industrial Revolution came along and changed everything.

Here, in the affluent West, we mostly use machines to do our heavy labor, we use cars and other transport to get us from place to place, we have leisure time when we sit for hours and take in a movie, watch TV, go to a show. The majority of modern jobs are desk-bound. Most of us don't need heavy meals because we don't expend that much physical energy.

But it's hard to break away from the way our forebears ate. We respect them, we look up to them, our instincts are to follow their example. But that's not working. Even the way of life of the post industrial revolution, as short a time ago as the Fifties, when people were full of post-war enthusiasm, isn't the right way of life for us at present.

The Fifties housewife prided herself on providing three full meals a day. Look at TV ads of the time and you'll see a smiling wife, her frilly apron covering her gingham dress, opening a fridge or oven door and proudly displaying loads of food.

Switch to another ad and her husband and children will be sitting at the dining-room table, beautifully laid. 'Mom' appears, carrying a magnificent turkey surrounded by roast potatoes, all displayed on a wonderful platter. A bowl heaped with vegetables is steaming on the table. There's enough to feed a family of twelve.

That was the ethos of the day, after the rationing and deprivations of WWII. It was the post-war idyll of plenteous food, domesticated women, placid children.

That scenario has changed dramatically. In most ordinary families both parents go out to work, at least once the children are past the toddler stage. Women's jobs are as time-consuming and demanding as men's; in fact they're the same job. There simply isn't time or energy for either parent to shop, then cook, then clean up.

This state of affairs produced a gap in the market and TV dinners appeared in supermarkets to fill it. Plain and unexciting at first, now you can buy cordon bleu meals, store them in the freezer, then you can microwave them, ready to serve up whenever family members are around for their meal. This means family members no longer have to eat at the same time, and often there isn't a particular time when everyone can get together. Dad's working late at the office, Mom's working out, and the kids have classes or are meeting friends.

There is another change. Portions of food served – at home or in restaurants – have virtually doubled since the 1950s. In their haste to serve the best bargains food chains have trained us to eat too much. Who needs a Supermac? Almost all of us would be better off with a Minimac, even if we had to pay the same price for it.

Of course – fortunately – we still need food. Lighter, less fatty food, and daintier food maybe. But we still need to eat to live, and we enjoy eating, we have appetites, meals are a large and enjoyable part of our lives. Not just at home – with friends and business associates, as well. We certainly wouldn't wish to do without food, even if there were a magic potion, taken once a day, which would take care of all that. Food isn't the problem – meals aren't the problem. The real problem is increasing weight for much of our society.

Perhaps what we should consider is whether there's a better, more appropriate, more contemporary way to enjoy our food – one which doesn't deprive us of enjoyment, but cuts down on the requirement for eating large amounts at one time.

So there we go – the **EATALL™** way is ideal for the whole family. All that's required is the right packaging, produced in small servings of whatever the people in a particular family enjoy. The following chapter, on **EATALL™ Cuisine,** gives some guidelines.

Raiding the icebox will no longer be considered a crime, it will be encouraged. As long as the portions are **EATALL™** size this way of eating is quick to prepare, instantly available, easily transportable; and there can be a wonderful choice. So there it is: the **EATALL™** way solves the problem of family meals, gives each member choices, fits into everyone's routine. Diverse tastes can be accommodated, and there will be less waste, less clearing up.

So what's the downside? Does it mean family members will never see each other, that they'll just sleep in the same house and meet in the kitchen occasionally?

Maybe that's a clue – meet in the kitchen, sit down with an **EATALL™** portion, a drink and a nice chat. Possibly there will be one or two snacks the family can all have together – the **EATALL™** way doesn't exclude family get-togethers, which can still be called meals. What it does is suggest that you 'graze' between meals, keep your body supplied with nutrients, and consequently eat much less at any timed or formal occasion.

This way of eating also gives parents the opportunity to provide healthy, as well as attractive, **EATALL™** portions for their children. They're going to snack anyway – do you know any kids that don't? Instead of bugging them, forbidding them, telling them they'll ruin their appetites for the next family meal, encourage them! You can use their natural, and wise, inclinations to feed them healthy **EATALL™** portions. And, because there will be so much more choice – a choice you've helped them make - the meals may well be much more attractive to your kids.

Maybe the whole family can get together to prepare **EATALL™** snacks for several days ahead. Most kids we know love helping in the kitchen. It's fun to invent new combinations, to work out the best way to store and offer the food.

Since **EATALL™** portions are meant to be small and varied the kids can make their own suggestions, they may even be able to cater to their own particular tastes without upsetting others at the 'meal'. It's a wonderful opportunity to give the kids a chance to be part of a new way of eating. It may even wean them off junk food. Now wouldn't that be something?

EATALL™ CUISINE

W e use the phrase **EATALL™ cuisine** to mean any method or ingredient which reduces the caloric content of meals, turning these into **EATALL™** portions with correspondingly fewer Calories, less fat and less sugar than conventional meals. **EATALL™ cuisine**, though by no means essential, will make losing weight even easier.

Rather than presenting you with a long list of recipes we've included some of our favorite **EATALL™** cooking methods in this chapter. These are simply recommendations for making **EATALL™** snacks. We've included fast methods for preparing food, and none of them require great cooking skills.

Please note that the following suggestions are not recipes; you do not need to know the exact amount of the ingredients, you need not even stick to them. What follows are cooking *methods* which can be adapted to suit your lifestyle, your cooking style and, eventually, your eating style.

Frying vegetables

Like fried onions? They're a wonderful food, fried to a deep golden brown. And they're supposed to protect you against cancer, as well… Think they're too heavy on the Calories to eat whenever you want? Try this:

Put a tablespoon of healthy oil (virgin olive oil, sunflower oil etc) for around one and a half pounds of sliced onions into a deep frying pan with a tight-fitting lid. Mix the onions with the oil, put on the lid, turn the heat to a low setting and sweat the onions until they're cooked to the consistency you like them.

Now take off the lid, turn up the heat and caramelize the onions;

this doesn't take long.

They taste, and look, as good as if they'd been fried in a lot of oil.

You don't have to stick to onions; try this method on potatoes, zucchini, egg plant, even apples. It's a great way to cook vegetables and some of the harder fruit.

Pâtés

Pâtés are a wonderful way to have a gastronomic experience which fits beautifully into the **EATALL™** way. They're expensive to buy but easy to make if you own a food processor. Bought ones have doubtful ingredients, including all kinds of preservatives. You don't need that.

All home-made pâtés can be stored in small containers for that single **EATALL™** portion – the tiny paper cups sold for home-made candies are excellent, but any small container will do. The paper cups hold about a heaped tablespoon. These small, individual pâtés can be frozen so you always have plenty on hand. And they're a wonderful way to use leftovers. The ingredients are entirely up to you. You don't have to use butter to blend them into a fine cream – you can use low-fat cream cheese instead. Philadelphia is one of the best.

Meat Pâtés

The tastiest ones are made of liver, but you can use leftover cooked meat if you like.

Buy some organic liver – chicken, lamb, ox, goose, pig – they all make fabulous pâtés. Fry the liver in a small amount of butter or a healthy oil until browned. Put everything into the food processor. Add herbs (parsley, sage, oregano, chervil, basil, whatever your favorite is) and blend until smooth. Add the contents of a 4 oz (100g) container of cream cheese, a raw egg or two. Blend. Now add carbohydrate (breadcrumbs, either brown or white, oat flakes, digestive biscuits, crackers) – enough to soak up excess moisture. Blend again. If the mixture is still too wet add more carbohydrate and blend once more. Spoon the mixture into small receptacles, set these in water in suitable containers and bake for 30 minutes at 350 F (170 C).

If you don't want the trouble of cooking the pâté just leave out the eggs or use hardboiled ones. And make sure the liver is cooked through before you blend. Then you can use the pâté straight from the processor. Store small amounts in suitable containers for future use. These pâtés will store in the refrigerator for three or four days, or you can put them in the freezer.

Fish Pâtés

These are easier to prepare than the liver pâtés because it's best to use pre-cooked or smoked ingredients. You can use the contents of tins of sardines or anchovy, smoked mackerel fillets with the skin removed, smoked trout, even smoked salmon if you like. Blend whatever you choose until smooth. Add a packet of low-fat cream cheese, and any herbs, spices and seasonings that you like. Blend again. Spoon into the paper cups, or other containers, and store.

Bean Pâtés

Adzuki beans give a wonderfully crunchy feel to bean pâtés. They're also said to be particularly healthy. Popular in the Far and Middle East, they're rich in soluble fiber which helps eliminate cholesterol from the body. They're also an abundant source of many minerals. Their high potassium and low sodium content give them the reputation of being able to reduce blood pressure.

Preparing your own adzuki beans requires a little work, but it's well worth the effort. Get some dried adzuki beans, soak them for at least four hours in twice their volume of water, rinse off the water. Now steam them, or boil them in water, for around thirty minutes.

Drain off any excess water, put them in a food processor and blend until well chopped. Add any other ingredients you like: fried onions as above, cooked or raw mushrooms, tomatoes, whatever you enjoy. Add flavorings of your choice – use seaweed instead of salt for a healthier option – add pepper and herbs of your choice, and blend all together. You can even blend in a vegetable bouillon cube for extra punch. The mixture tastes fantastic and can be stored like the meat and fish pâtés given above.

You don't have to stick to adzuki beans – you can use any bean for this pâté . Buy tinned beans to save time and energy. The texture will be smoother and perhaps not quite as tasty. If the mixture is too soggy add some carbohydrate, as above.

Nut Butters

Seeds, nuts and peanuts can easily be made into smooth or chunky butters.

Take one cup of roasted nuts, add a tablespoon and a half of any good oil, blend everything until you have a paste. Make it as smooth or chunky as you prefer. You may need to scrape the mixture from the edges of the bowl from time to time. Lighten with cream cheese or yogurt.

Tahini

Sesame seeds can readily be made into tahini. Just roast a cup of shelled seeds on a baking tray in the oven, grind the roasted seeds in a blender, add a little water plus around a quarter cup of any good oil of your choice. The result is a simple, flavorful. paste which supplies many vitamins and minerals. Tahini also makes an excellent addition to any sauces or dressings.

Blue Poppy Seeds

Many blenders have a grinder attachment you can use for coffee beans or small, hard seeds. Half fill the container with poppy seeds and grind them until they're the texture of ground almonds. The ground seeds can be cooked with a very small amount of water and sugar to make a wonderfully nutritious filling for strudels.

Cheese and Cheese Spread

Cheese is a high-density food and is, therefore, best eaten in small quantities. Grate some hard cheese – tasty cheddar, Parmesan, Emmenthaler, any hard cheese of your choice – and store it in a Ziploc™ bag in your refrigerator. Sprinkle or mix it into food; you'll have all the taste without the heavy Calories.

Non-fat cottage cheese can be used as a base to make a delicious cheese spread with all the piquancy of a blue cheese but without so many Calories.

Take a small tub of non-fat cottage cheese; add 2 oz (50g) Danish Blue and 2 oz (50g) of Philadelphia Lite. Blend all these ingredients and store in small containers. These will make a perfect **EATALL™** portion which can be combined with fruit, vegetables or salad.

Burgers

It's very simple to make your own burgers, and you'll know precisely how lean your meat content is. Buy the leanest beef you can find. It doesn't have to be steak, shank actually has more flavor and is much cheaper. Put it in your food processor to chop. Add finely chopped, or caramelized, onions for good flavor, add chopped garlic if you like it, then add seaweed flakes, tamari sauce and pepper. Add any other seasonings you enjoy. Take the mixture out of the processor, add some fine breadcrumbs and mix everything together thoroughly. Shape the mixture into patties, put them onto a lightly-oiled grill, or fry them in a non-stick pan. Another method is to put the mixture into small muffin trays, or to use the flexible, non-stick kind. You can also use paper cups, choosing the size used for baking cupcakes. Just pat the mixture down into these shapes. Grill, broil or bake the burgers for five to seven minutes.

After cooking the burgers in the paper cups will be particularly easy to store. Put them into plastic bags in the fridge or freezer; each mini burger will make a splendid **EATALL™** portion when teamed with a salad.

Creamed Vegetable Soups

A delicious, creamy soup can be made from any king of vegetable, but Brussels sprouts make one of the best.

The amounts vary with the size of your blender. Assuming one with a capacity of 2.5 pints (1500 ml), buy 1 lb (.5 kilo) of Brussels sprouts, peel them and steam them until quite soft. Fill one half of the blender glass with the steamed sprouts, then add enough hot water to fill two thirds of the glass. Pulse until the sprouts are mashed, then blend until the mixture is quite smooth. If the mixture appears too thick, add more hot liquid. You can use cream or yogurt for part or all of the liquid if you prefer.

Now add any flavorings you favor; a vegetable bouillon cube makes a piquant addition, but it does cover the taste of the sprouts.

The soup is very creamy and quite delicious, and is often enjoyed by people who don't actually like sprouts or other vegetables. You can substitute leeks, onions, carrots, sweet potato, or a mixture of whatever vegetables you enjoy. Remember to cut any root vegetables into small chunks to cut down the time needed for steaming, and to make the blending easier.

Any left-over soup can be stored in the refrigerator for two or three days.

Cabbage delights

Cabbage is good for you. It has lots of fiber to help digestion, it's said to be good for avoiding cancer, it's cheap and plentiful to buy. Treated the right way it's enjoyable to eat and makes a great snack.

Get some organic, white or red, firm cabbage. Slice it into thin strips using a food processor attachment, or by hand (make sure the slices are thin). Put **EATALL™** portions into Ziploc™ bags and store in the refrigerator. The cabbage is great to nibble on – and an excellent health food.

Put some of the slices in a bowl, adding a small amount of water and caraway seeds. Now steam for about fifteen minutes. The cabbage will still be crisp, and will have a different flavor. Store in Ziploc™ bags as before.

Cooked red cabbage makes a really tasty dish which is great eaten in small quantities, just like a pickle. Chop a small red cabbage in your food processor – no need to slice. Add a cup of cider vinegar, a tablespoon of sugar, a handful of raisins, a chopped apple or two. Cook in a covered dish in the microwave for around twenty minutes. If the mixture is runny blend a tablespoon of cornflower with some water and add it to the cabbage. Microwave for another five minutes.

This dish is a wonderful accompaniment to meat in a traditional meal, but it's also a very tasty **EATALL™** portion. It keeps, in a covered bowl in the refrigerator, for up to ten days. Use it hot or cold. Add chestnuts to vary the flavor.

Mixed Bean Salad

Open a can of mixed beans. Place them in a strainer and rinse off the juices under running water. Let the beans drain, then place them in a bowl. Add a small, finely chopped onion or two chopped shallots, two tablespoons of virgin olive oil, the juice of three lemons and chopped herbs and seasonings to taste. Mix the ingredients with a spatula, cover the bowl and allow the salad to season in the refrigerator for a few hours. Serve at room temperature.

A refreshing dressing for a bean salad is yogurt. Take some herbs, such as parsley or coriander, chop them finely and combine with the yogurt. Now mix the cooked beans in that.

Two tablespoons of either of these simple salads make a very good and nourishing **EATALL™** portion. Spoon the bean mixture over some fresh lettuce leaves or any other green salad leaves.

Mashed Vegetables

Mashed potatoes taste wonderful – well, the right kind of mashed potatoes do. A creamy potato variety cooked until it's soft, mixed with hot milk and butter, seasoned, creamed in a food mixer – fantastic. But it's a heavy ingredient for an **EATALL™** portion.

Try substituting yams, rutabagas, turnips, carrots and particularly celeriac for the potatoes. Mash the steamed-soft vegetables in a blender rather than a food processor to make a smooth paste. This even works with Brussels sprouts. You don't need milk because the vegetables hold a lot of liquid compared to potatoes. Mix in some seasonings, a little butter or low-fat cream cheese. Blend at high speed to make the mixture light. Wonderful.

If you miss the texture of potato try a half-and-half mixture. It's lighter than mashed potato and quite delightful. Blend the vegetables first, then combine them with potatoes mashed in a food processor. Add a little low-fat creamed cheese or milk if the mixture is too stiff.

Salsa

Salsa is the Spanish, Arabic, and Italian word meaning any kind of *sauce*. In English it usually refers to the spicy, often tomato-based, dips generally used with Mexican food.

It's easy to make up your own salsa recipe. The basic one is made of chopped, raw tomatoes mixed with sweet peppers, a little onion, and any herbs you enjoy. Just put your favorite mixture in your food processor and blend. Add yogurt if it's too spicy for your taste, or add a little cream cheese to make a change.

A wonderful site for a huge number of salsa recipes is:

http://www.recipe-ideas.co.uk/salsa-recipes.htm

Let your imagination vary the ingredients, or simply use up any vegetables you have handy. We like to store a covered dish in the refrigerator and mix a tablespoon into a stored **EATALL™** portion which may have become dull.

Guacamole

This is just salsa with avocado added. The trick here is to make the salsa in the food processor, then cut the avocado into chunks and mix these in manually rather than blending them in.

Be sure to refrigerate any salsa you want to keep for several days.

Gravies and Sauces

Roast meat without gravy is too dry, steamed fish too plain. And what is the use of boiled asparagus or artichokes without mayonnaise? And what about the dipping sauces for Thai, Japanese and Chinese food?

All these can be prepared and stored in small amounts. Ketchup and mustard are already being produced commercially in this way, though it would be helpful to see ketchup without too much sugar... You may prefer to make your own so that these condiments won't contain any questionable additives. Home-made sauces can also contain fewer Calories. Not that you can't use traditional sauces and gravies when using the **EATALL™** way to slim, but if you're trying to take off weight rapidly these lighter sauces could help.

Basically you replace a thickening agent with a steamed, then blended, vegetable or fruit purée. The sauce will not only have far fewer Calories, it will gain in taste and nutrition as well.

Salad Dressings

Ordinary French dressing is quite heavy on Calories. There are several simple alternatives which can taste as good or better, and which will make sure your **EATALL™** portion is not too heavy on Calories.

Lemon juice, milk and sugar

Instead of using oil and vinegar, try using lemon juice, milk and a little sugar. Sounds unlikely, doesn't it? But it works.

Wash your salad leaves; this dressing is particularly good with lettuce. Squeeze the juice from three lemons, mix it with a little sugar, and then add half a cup of milk. Mix well, and then pour it over the salad.

Mayonnaise

Making your own mayonnaise using a blender is simplicity itself. However, instead of using oil to make it you can substitute plain yogurt for your dressing, or use evaporated milk thickened with lemon juice. Then simply add seasonings and spices of your choice. This mixture will contain a quarter of the Calories of any mayonnaise made with olive oil.

Fruit juice dressings

Different fruit juices can be used to make interesting dressings. Pomegranate makes an unusual dressing, as does cranberry. If you combine a cup of any fruit juice with roughly three teaspoons of Balsamic vinegar, then blend with one tablespoon of mustard and any herbs, spices or other seasonings you and enjoy. Now add some virgin olive oil; a quarter of a cup should be plenty. Mix all together for an unusual dressing which is low in calories compared to French dressing.

Banana Cream

This cream was invented in the 1970s. It became a firm family favorite, is Blitzkrieg quick to make, and always impresses guests.

Put one or two ripe bananas into your food processor, add one tin of full-cream evaporated milk and blend until smooth. This is the basic cream. Now add as little sugar as possible for your personal taste – you'll be surprised how little you need once you get used to it.

The last ingredient is lemon juice. This can be bottled or freshly squeezed. The amount depends on the amount of banana you use, but the juice from four or five lemons should be ample. Any leftover lemon juice will keep in the refrigerator for several days.

Set the machine on to a slow spin. Now dribble the lemon juice on to the mixture until it begins to thicken – similar to making mayonnaise. Increase the speed. You're looking for the consistency of whipped cream.

When the mixture thickens stop the machine and pour the banana cream into small containers of your choice. It will set almost immediately into a thick custard cream. Store it in the fridge for up to four hours. After that it tends to separate.

Serve this mixture with fruit, or cheesecake, or anything that's good with a cream. This recipe has less than half the Calories of an equivalent amount of whipped cream. Remember to use **EATALL™** portions; the quantity given makes about ten.

The Original Muesli

The supermarkets offer many choices of cereal they call muesli. However, all these are actually dry cereals combined with some nuts and dried fruit; they come in various mixtures.

The original muesli is a fresh fruit dish. It is usually made with an apple, combined with oat flakes or porridge oats, nuts, honey, a tablespoon of milk and a little lemon juice; milk or yogurt can be added at the end to adjust the consistency.

Put a heaped tablespoon of any kind of flaked or rolled oats you enjoy into your food processor. Add an apple cut into rough chunks, plus the juice of half a lemon, add a little honey, 4 or 5 almonds, and a tablespoon or two of milk or yogurt, depending on which type of oat flakes you use. Some are drier than others. Now blend all these ingredients, but don't overdo it – the muesli should be chunky.

You'll end up with a fresh, zingy cereal dish which should taste more of apple than of oats. Try it; you'll be surprised how delicious it is, and how much fresher it tastes than a dry breakfast cereal.

You could soak the rolled oats in the milk overnight for a muesli with a softer consistency. And you can also vary the ingredients as you wish: use a pear instead of an apple, walnuts instead of almonds.

Be adventurous, it's more fun that way. After a while you may not even want to add the honey; the mixture will taste too sweet.

The quantities given make at least two good **EATALL™** portions. Don't be tempted to make more to store for the next day. This is a dish which needs to be eaten freshly blended.

Small Dishes

An excellent way to limit the amount you eat is to place a portion on a bread plate rather than on a dinner plate or, if appropriate, use a very small bowl. Another way to get the idea that you are eating rather more than you actually are is to use a cake fork or a teaspoon instead of ordinary cutlery.

IDEAL EATALL™ FOODS

We've emphasized that you can eat any type of food using the EATALL™ way, and that is true. However, since you will be eating such small portions, we'd like to draw your attention to some of the most nutritional foods you can buy.

Super Foods

For healthier weight loss consider eating some of the 'healthy', sometimes called 'super foods', which happen to appeal to you. While these may be more expensive, that is less of a concern when you're eating so much less at any one time. Caviar, for example, is one of our favorites. If you particularly like it the small amounts used for an EATALL™ portion can become a staple in your EATALL™ way of eating.

Sashimi is another expensive, and small-portioned, food which can provide treats when eating the EATALL™ way.

Different authorities list different foods as super foods. For example, Dr Stephen Pratt, of the Pratt Lab, School of Life Sciences, Arizona State University, lists fourteen foods he thinks are wonderful: beans, blueberries, broccoli, oats, oranges, pumpkins, salmon, soy, spinach, tea (green or black) tomatoes, turkey, walnuts and yogurt.

Nicholas Perricone, MD, FACN, is a research dermatologist, and CEO of NV Perricone MD, Ltd. His list of ten super foods is: Acai berry, anything in the alliums family such as onions or garlic, green foods, buckwheat, beans, hot peppers, nuts and seeds, yogurt and kefir.

Other authorities list different foods and, as you'll be eating such small quantities, you may find it useful to seek them out and incorporate them into your EATALL™ portions.

Then there are the Omega-3 and Omega-6 essential fatty acids, said to be needed not only for your health but also for losing weight. The latest fad is extra virgin coconut oil, said to be superior to any other oil for cooking.

The best vegetable oils are said to be:

Omega 3 oils:
linseed oil, walnut oil, canola oil, soybean oil, wheat germ oil

Omega 6 oils:
Safflower oil, grape seed oil, sunflower oil, walnut oil, soybean oil and corn oil.

Mixed oils:
Linseed oil
Extra Virgin coconut oil

Some authorities even claim you need to have at least a tablespoon of oil a day to lose weight. Others insist that vegetable oils aren't good enough.

They consider fish oils to be the best sources for these Omega 3 and Omega 6 oils:

Fish oils:
cod liver oil, halibut liver oil, krill oil

You've heard all that, but even here opinions are divided. The purest fish oil is said to come from a fish called Hoki.

Many of these super foods are undoubtedly excellent sources of nutrition, but it isn't quite as simple as that. Farmed salmon can, for example, be of doubtful benefit, so try to get wild salmon if you can.

You probably already know which foods are good for you, and that you should opt for organic if you can. You'll be cutting down on the amounts of food you eat at each 'meal', so you can afford to be much choosier, both in health and in dollar terms. Our point is that if you're eating the **EATALL™** way, which involves much smaller quantities for each **EATALL™** portion than eating the normal way, it's worth being particularly fussy about your food.

Keep an open mind, and just try to eat the healthiest food you can find. It makes sense, and you can afford it for small portions.

Fruit

Fruit is a wonderful source of vitamins and fiber. Unfortunately many fruits are heavily laden with sugar.

The **highest sugar-carriers** are:

> bananas, pomegranates, cherries, pineapples, watermelons, litchis, kiwis, persimmons, figs, grapes and, surprisingly, apples.

All the tastiest ones, right? This doesn't mean you cannot eat them when eating the **EATALL™** way – remember, nothing is forbidden. We're just drawing your attention to the facts, so that you can substitute a less sugary fruit if you like it equally well.

There are plenty of others: the citrus family, tomatoes, avocados, berries. There's nothing you cannot enjoy, but you do need to know that many fruits carry a high loading of sugar. So, eat them, but keep the portion size small, or choose a smaller portion later that day.

Dried Fruit

All dried fruit is delicious, but unfortunately it's sugar-laden and the **EATALL™** portion will be, at most, a very small handful. You can buy raisins in small packages, but these are really too sweet and therefore too Calorie-laden for one **EATALL™** portion. However, it's a simple matter to buy packages from health shops – they come in as little as 4 oz (100g) packs – and divide these into four. Use small, Ziploc™ plastic bags to keep your portions in.

The choice of dried food is amazing:

dates, raisins, currants, cherries, banana chips, figs, apples, cranberries, blueberries, diced pineapple, mango strips, apricots, prunes, guava, mango, papaya, strawberries, peaches, pears

No doubt there are many more. Doesn't reading this list make your mouth water? Enjoy, but stick to your **EATALL™** portions

Raw Vegetables

Cherry tomatoes, baby carrots, bell peppers cored and cut into eighths, radishes, young turnips cut into quarters, mushrooms, rutabagas cut into roughly bite-size chunks, snow peas, celery cut into 3-inch sticks, small cucumbers, large cucumbers cut into bite-size wedges, spring onions cut to within four inches of the bulb are all outstanding ingredients for an **EATALL™** portion . Cauliflower cut into rosettes, and broccoli cut in the same way, add crunch. Red or white cabbage can be thin-sliced and added to a veggie mix or even used on its own. Some people enjoy raw onion rings – bear in mind that onions come in many different strengths, from mild to ultra pungent.

All the vegetables listed make excellent choices to put into small plastic bags or other containers. Enclose whatever takes your fancy of the above, mixed in any way you like, for a raw veggie **EATALL™**

portion of food with real nutritional kick. If you find the thought of mixed raw vegetables just too much you could add some fruit to the mix – avoid the sugar-laden ones, but pomegranate seeds, blueberries and strawberries might make the mixture more attractive to you.

Cooked Vegetables

Don't like raw vegetables? Use cooked, instead. What you lose in nutrients you gain in Calorie bulk – cooked vegetables have fewer Calories than raw ones.

Some varieties of vegetable, like beetroot, generally only taste good when cooked, though there are varieties that can be delicious eaten raw. The squash family, too, is usually preferred cooked, though people living in England during WWII used the flesh of young squashes, raw, as a substitute for melons which don't mature easily in that climate.

Many plants of the cabbage family are also better served cooked. Potatoes should not be eaten raw, nor should plantain, yam, and sweet potato. Remember all these are dense in carbohydrates, so keep the portions small.

Salad Vegetables

You know what they are, and that there is an enormous choice. Any kind of lettuce, endive, spinach, grated root vegetables, sliced edible fungi, sprouted seeds as well as fruits like tomatoes and avocado. These all make excellent salad ingredients. Mix your favorites and keep several portions handy. You'll find it difficult to eat too much salad because of the bulk, so go ahead, splurge and feel virtuous, healthy and slim.

A number of cooked root vegetables make excellent salads. Old carrots cooked until they are still a little hard, cooked beetroot sliced, covered in cider vinegar with some caraway seeds added. And whether a salad is tasty or not depends, to a large extent, on the dressing used. Salad dressings were discussed in the chapter on **EATALL™ cuisine.**

Legumes & other Large Seeds

Consider all kinds of legumes:

---

raw, shelled peas and broad beans, any other raw beans you enjoy eating; sweet corn kernels cooked or raw, peanuts

---

The list includes peanuts because they are a legume.

There is an enormous choice of beans, all best cooked, some of which are listed here:

---

adzuki, mung, kidney, lima, black-eyed, garbanzo, cranberry, navy, pinto, small red, red lentils, green lentils

---

For your **EATALL™** time you might like to combine two or three tablespoons of these cooked legumes with chopped herbs you enjoy, with chopped onions if you like raw onion, with any of the vegetables listed above. Then add carbohydrates and fiber in a pleasingly tasty form. Top or toss with your favorite dressing.

Smaller Seeds

Pumpkin, sunflower, sesame and poppy seeds are stocked by most super-markets and all health stores. The first two can be eaten raw, used like nuts in your **EATALL™** portions or sprinkled over salads. Sesame and poppy seeds are best used for cooking or baking, as already mentioned in **EATALL™ cuisine**.

Nuts

Nuts are seeds protected by a hard shell. They're excellent sources of protein, vitamins A and E, several minerals such as phosphorous and potassium, as well as fiber. They're very good for your health as well as delicious to eat. They also provide unique taste and texture experiences, making fantastic additions to **EATALL™** portions even when used in small quantities.

The best-known, readily available nuts are:

Walnuts, almonds, hazelnuts, pistachios, pecans, macadamias, pine nuts, Brazil nuts, cashews and coconuts.

All these can be eaten raw, though the coconut will have to be broken up into **EATALL™** portions.

Sweet chestnuts are delicious too. They have fewer calories than other nuts but have a bitter after-taste when eaten raw. They can be boiled, to use with vegetables or to add to stuffing for meats. As a snack they are delicious roasted. A small paper bag of roasted chestnuts is a common offering from street vendors in northern European countries in the winter. They make an unusual **EATALL™** portion and warm your hands at the same time.

Because nuts are high in carbohydrate and oils, and therefore Calorie rich, it's expedient to only use a small handful for your **EATALL™** portion. A good way to enjoy their taste without over-loading on Calories is to mix them with sprouted seeds. You might like to try walnuts with sprouted alfalfa, hazelnuts with sprouted mung beans, brazil nuts mixed with the tangy taste of mustard seed. The combinations are unusual, exciting and a wonderful contribution to a healthy lifestyle. Store your favorite blend in a small bag in the refrigerator, but only for a day or two.

Sprouted Seeds

Sprouted seeds are considered one of the healthiest foods available. They can be grown at home, without soil and with very little trouble. They will reward you with cheap, abundant, healthful vitamins, minerals and amino acids. The phenomenal advantages claimed for them are expounded on several websites. Enough here to suggest the types of seeds to sprout, and to suggest you include them in as many **EATALL™** portions as you can manage.

There are more pluses: the seeds take only between 1-14 days to sprout and yield between twice to eight times their volume. The seed shelf life is between 1-10 years and the sprouted seed shelf-life between 1-6 weeks. A real bargain.

One site on the internet offers eighty varieties of seed, so you'll never get bored.

http://www.sproutpeople.com/

Mix the sprouted seeds with any of the vegetables listed above. They're also outstanding in sandwiches or mixed into butters of various types.

The usual seeds to sprout are:

---

alfalfa and clover for leaf sprouts, mung, lentil, peas and many bean varieties for a nutty taste, broccoli, cabbage, radish, mustard and cress and other brassica sprouts for cancer protection, wheat, barley, rye, all nuts and seeds listed above, garlic and onion, fenugreek, arugula, flax.

Cereals

You already know you can buy single-portion cereal packages of the most popular kinds. Adding non-fat milk won't increase the Calorie count by too much, and the exact nutrition facts for each package are neatly displayed on it. These packs make an ideal **EATALL™** portion for the first **EATALL™** time of the day. They're also great for people who enjoy eating cereal several times during the day.

One way to increase bulk without adding many Calories is to add bran. This is available from health stores, and you can buy wheat, oat, rice and several other bran products. Bran is the insoluble part of vegetable matter. It doesn't add many Calories to the food, but it does add fiber and bulk, both of which are excellent for good digestion.

There's nothing to stop you adding fruit to your cereal – berries, bananas, dried fruit are all healthful additions. Nuts are also useful. Just remember that each **EATALL™** portion is meant to be small, so if you add fruit and/or nuts you need to consider decreasing the amount of cereal. If you want to add Calorie-laden dried fruit it might be best to find single-portion packages of muesli, so you can tell how much you're actually eating. As before, find a very small bowl and eat the cereal with a teaspoon.

Enjoy porridge? You can buy an instant mix and prepare it in a small bowl for an **EATALL™** portion – just be careful as many of those mixes have a lot of sugar in them. Or you can cook your own porridge made from rolled oats, eat a single portion, and keep the rest in suitably small containers you can microwave later.

Bread & Cakes

Bread used to be called 'the staff of life'. At a time when hard, physical labor was the norm bread filled the hungry stomach and was a wonderful food. It was also wholegrain. Much of the bread now sold, usually prepackaged, is simply a spongy mass of sugar with little nutritional value. If you enjoy this type of bread, eat it sparingly if possible. It's your choice. But limit yourself to one slice at each **EATALL™** time if you can.

As you know bread combines well with many foods. Sandwiches are a great way to package **EATALL™** portions for taking to the office, on a picnic, whatever. Instead of two slices of bread to make one sandwich cut one slice in half and use these two halves to make one sandwich. Fill sandwiches with any of the foods listed above. You *can* use butter, but you don't have to. And you can spread it thinly rather than lather it on.

Slip a small sandwich made with meat, fish, egg, whatever takes your fancy into a Ziploc™ bag, add some salad. You'll have an excellent **EATALL™** portion.

Cakes are hard to resist. Don't deprive yourself completely. Eat a small slice – you know the size – eat it slowly, savor it. A small amount tastes just as good as a huge helping.

Meat and Fish

Meat and fish contain large amounts of available protein so, if you want to indulge in a large meal, go for lean meat. For **EATALL™** portions be a little more selective: one crisp rasher of bacon plus a handful of vegetables, a small slice of calf liver with fried onions, two chicken livers with a tossed salad, a small chicken leg, or breast, or wing. All these can be used in the **EATALL™** way. Use the leanest cuts you can find, use any type of meat you're happy with.

Sashimi is a boon for the **EATALL™** way. Three or four of the portions served by most restaurants are fine. Enjoy a variety of fish, eat the grated radish it's served with. Avoid the rice if you can, but eat it if you must in small amounts and over a longer time.

Fish roe – caviar when obtained from sturgeon living in the Black Sea – is an excellent food. The **EATALL™** portion is small enough to allow for the occasional caviar treat, but 'false' caviar from whitefish, pike, cod, trout and salmon is also delicious. Any of these can be cooked, and scrambled with eggs, to make a double **EATALL™** portion. Share with a friend.

Cheese

If you like cheese you can use it to flavor all kinds of **EATALL™** portions. Though it doesn't contain sugar cheese is a dense food, much of it heavy on fat. It's easy to eat too much at one sitting, and the packaging usually holds more than is useful for one **EATALL™** portion. As already mentioned, a simple solution for hard cheeses is to flake or grate them. Combined with other food – like salad or hot vegetables – they give the **EATALL™** portion the taste of cheese without overloading your body.

Does that mean you can never enjoy the soft cheeses, such as camembert, Roquefort, brie and Stilton? Of course not. Take small amounts when sharing a meal with friends, or cut a small piece and dribble or crumble it over other food. Don't deny yourself any food – just learn to savor small amounts.

There is one form of cheese which has very little or no fat – cottage cheese. You can eat half a cup for an **EATALL™** portion and combine it with salad, or vegetables, or fruit. If you use it as a base for a cheese spread, as given in **EATALL™ cuisine,** you can have the taste of a much denser cheese without the Calories.

Eggs

A soft-boiled, fried or scrambled egg makes a perfect **EATALL™** portion. Use the small size eggs for a small portion. Add herbs to make a tasty omelet, or be liberal with mushrooms. Even more simply, hard-boil several eggs so they're ready for an **EATALL™** egg portion whenever you feel like one.

You don't have to stick to chicken eggs. Duck eggs have a creamier taste, goose eggs need to be shared but quail eggs are tiny. Two or three make a tasty, and different, **EATALL™** snack.

Chocolate

It isn't the chocolate which is so bad for you – it's the high sugar content of much chocolate confectionary. Notice we're talking about chocolate – bar chocolate – not chocolates, which come in a fancy box and have higher sugar content.

If you're a real chocoholic you can learn to love the 70% plus cocoa solids chocolate bars on the market now. You can even buy one with 99% cocoa solids. Some have small amounts of flavoring added: mint, orange, ginger – or are mixed with nuts. The bars come marked into sections. Open the packaging, break the bar into its sections, eat one only at a time. A rough estimate of small squares is around 25 Calories each. Allow the chocolate to melt, slowly, on your tongue. That's really all there is to say about that. One or two pieces of chocolate make an enjoyable **EATALL™** portion which is small enough to be eaten surreptitiously.

These suggestions are all you need to choose the most practical ingredients for your **EATALL™** 'meals'. In the next chapter we suggest how to prepare the most practical **EATALL™** portions. But don't forget: the main point is to remember to eat.

IDEAL EATALL™ PORTIONS

The most practical size for **EATALL™** portions is made up of roughly 100-150 Calories. This is the most convenient measurement for the average sized person. If you're larger, or normally consume many more Calories, you can increase that amount by half, or even double it. If you're smaller, or normally consume many less Calories, you can decrease the amount. Eventually a person of average size won't want to eat more than approximately 100 Calories at each **EATALL™** time because the slimmer body will simply not need more. This is not to suggest that you count Calories – it's more a question of getting an idea how much is sufficient, and Calories are the most convenient way of expressing this throughout the food groups. An excellent site to answer all your Calorie questions is;

www.Calorie-count.com.

We've put together some ideas for **EATALL™** portions that you might like to eat for those twelve to seventeen times you'll eat during the day. They give you a wonderful opportunity to savor a whole host of different foods.

The suggestions below are given in roughly 100 Calorie portions. However, it certainly isn't necessary to stick to 100 Calories at all times. You can vary the amount from 50 to 250 Calories each time you eat, just try not to exceed your normal daily caloric consumption. When others are enjoying a meal, and you would like to join them, you might find yourself eating 250 Calories or even more. Just cut down your portions appropriately at your other eating times. The whole point of the **EATALL™** method is its flexibility, in the fact you do not have to count Calories or are not allowed some foods.

If you enjoy snack foods you'll find the supermarkets already carry many packages ideal for providing one or several **EATALL™**

portions. We're not saying that these foods are the healthiest, or the most nutritious, choices you can make – but that's strictly for you to decide. The point is that they're there for you, conveniently packaged and ready to eat.

There's a huge variety to choose from, so if you wish to use any of these packages for your **EATALL™** portion you're certainly not deprived of choice. You can find small packages of chips, crackers, cookies, soups, sauces, breads, cakes, cheeses, meats, yogurts, jellies, beef jerky, hot dogs,. smoked fish – you get the idea. Most of these packages hold too much for a single **EATALL™** portion, but only for the present time. Once the idea catches on the smaller packaging will soon follow.

If you're into health foods, we've provided a list of healthy options which are not confined to fanatic type eating, and if you have a sweet tooth – as we do – there are fantastic choices for you to try out.

It's worth mentioning again that, though you certainly don't want to be counting Calories, many **EATALL™** portions come out at around the 100 Calorie mark. So, if you're eating seventeen of these a day, you'll be consuming a very reasonable amount of 1700 Calories. You can afford to double up at conventional meal times which stretch over an hour period, just to make it easier to comply with the **EATALL™** way.

As already mentioned, because you'll be eating relatively small amounts of food at any one time you might like to consider the nutritional value quite carefully. Some suggestions about this are given in each category.

The first in the list of **EATALL™** portions is a combination of protein and vegetables. You can use any type of protein and any kind of vegetable. So fish, meat, cheese, eggs, Soya and other bean products are all in this group. All the given combinations are simple to prepare and easy to carry around in a Ziploc™ bag.

We're offering a few suggestions to get you started. However, it's very important that you really enjoy your **EATALL™** portions, so do make up your own.

A Vegetable and Cheese EATALL™ Portion

Portion: A deseeded, half shell of pepper filled with cheese.

One large bell pepper has around 40 Calories. The amounts vary between red, green and yellow, but hardly significantly for our purpose

A 1in (2.5cm) cube of full-fat cheese has roughly 80 Calories

Cottage cheese, and reduced fat cheese, has fewer Calories. You can use half a cup of cottage cheese, and two 1in (2.5cm) cubes of reduced-fat cheese if you wish.

This portion is very easy to assemble, it can be varied by using different types of cheese, and it can also be made using the **Cheese Spread** mentioned in the chapter on **EATALL™ Cuisine.**

Of course you don't need to stick to bell peppers. Celery sticks, cucumbers, tomatoes (classed as both a fruit and a vegetable), salad leaves, carrots, radishes – any raw vegetable you enjoy can be substituted, just as different cheeses can be substituted.

A Vegetable and Meat EATALL™ Portion

Portion: A salad vegetable eaten with slices of meat or pâté.

To vary the vegetable and protein portion you can substitute meat, or meat products.

A couple of thin slices of lean ham, one slice of pastrami or four slices of chicken breast combined with a salad vegetable will make an excellent **EATALL™** portion.

Meats vary widely in their caloric content. For example 4 oz (100g) of white turkey meat will be 130 Calories, whereas 4 oz (100g) of topside roast beef will come in at 215 Calories. If you have a special preference you may wish to check the food on:

www.Calorie-count.com

and decide on the portion which is right for you.

You very quickly get a feel for what you need.

A Vegetable and Fish EATALL™ Portion

Portion: A salad vegetable combined with fish or fish pâté .

You can vary the vegetable and protein **EATALL™** portion even more by substituting fish for the protein part of the portion. Use freshly cooked fish, smoked fish, canned fish or fish pâté. All these make excellent **EATALL™** portions, but again vary considerably in caloric content. For example a half tin of sardines in tomato sauce is only around 70 Calories, while the same amount in olive oil is around 100 Calories. Shell fish is generally lower in Calories than ordinary fish, but again substitution lists are easily found on the web. The point is that there is ample choice, so go ahead, enjoy.

A Vegetable and Egg EATALL™ Portion

Portion: 1 hen egg eaten with a cracker, a few potato crisps or a vegetable portion

This **EATALL™** portion is particularly easy to prepare. An egg has around 80 Calories, give or take a few. A duck egg has around 130 Calories, a goose egg around 240.

Eggs can be boiled, scrambled, fried or made into an omelet. Use only a small amount of butter, olive oil or healthy margarine in the base of a non-stick frying pan to avoid Calorie overload. You can always share a goose egg omelet with someone else, or hard-boil the egg and use a half or a quarter for each **EATALL™** portion.

The Calorie values of eggs cooked in various ways are detailed at
www.thecaloriecounter.com
as well as on many other sites. It is interesting to contrast two boiled eggs, coming in at 160 Calories ,with the **Two Egg Mushrooms and Muenster** breakfast on the menu in some restaurants. It comes in at a whacking 728 Calories. This is merely to illustrate that you need to be alert to changes in caloric values when using different cooking methods.

A Vegetable and Bean EATALL™ Portion

Portion: ½ cup beans served with low-Calorie vegetables.

Beans can be prepared as a healthful salad, with French dressing replaced by lemon juice flavored with spices or fresh herbs. Add chopped onions if you like raw onions. See the **EATALL™ Cuisine** chapter for a delicious mixed-bean salad.

A ½ cup of canned beans is roughly 100 Calories. Combine this with a leaf salad for a nutritious **EATALL™** portion. The bean pâté given in **EATALL™ Cuisine** is excellent combined with vegetables.

Vegetable Dishes & Salads

Portion: ½ a cup of raw vegetables, combined with a cup of salad vegetables, all tossed in a low-Calorie dressing, will make a filling EATALL™ portion.

You might like to prepare an **EATALL™** portion which consists purely of vegetables. No problem. Here is one suggestion, but of course you can choose any kinds vegetables or salads you prefer, and you can choose to combine raw or cooked vegetables. This type of **EATALL™** portion will be the bulkiest if composed of green vegetables, since most of these are low in Calories but high in bulk. You need to bear in mind that root and tuber vegetables are much higher in Calories: that is potatoes, sweet potatoes, carrots and so on.

Mixed salad: half a cup of snow peas, one cup of diced tomato, one half cup of diced cucumber, one cup shredded salad leaves.

Mix all the ingredients and toss them in a low-Calorie dressing. You may find it hard to eat your way through this amount.

There is a huge number of permutations for salads or hot vegetable dishes – it really all depends on your personal taste. What holds true in general is that, for most people, a variety of vegetables served together will be more appealing than just a single one. Choose your favorites, bag up some **EATALL™** portions, and enjoy.

Bread & Sandwiches

Portion: A slice of bread topped by a slice of meat, fish or cheese. A sandwich made using a slice of bread halved with any filling of your choice.

On average a slice of bread is around 80 Calories. Halve it, add a filling and place the other half on top, and you have an **EATALL™** portion sandwich. It will be difficult to find fillings with less than 50 Calories, so consider a sandwich one of your larger **EATALL™** portions. Think along the lines of 150 Calories and you can fill your bread with a hardboiled egg, slices of cold meat or cheese, pâtés of various kinds, smoked fish – anything you enjoy, as long as you remember to keep the fillings within reasonable limits.

Brown bread has no fewer Calories than white bread – well, not significantly. What you may find is that a slice of whole grain bread is more satisfying than one of white bread, and that you'll come to prefer it.

Breakfast Cereals

Portion: 1 cup of cereal eaten with ½ a cup of non-fat milk, topped with a few berries.

Alternatively, eat a small cup of the Natural Muesli mentioned in the EATALL™ Cuisine chapter.

There are a number of cereals which you can buy in mini boxes which hold roughly 100 Calories. These are not exact amounts, those really aren't necessary. Just remember that when you add milk you add Calories, and need to take that into account. If you add full cream milk, or even cream, that will, of course, increase the number of Calories substantially.

Half a mini box of cereal, plus half a cup of non-fat milk, with a few berries thrown in for flavor, would make an excellent **EATALL™** portion.

Cakes, Pies & Pastries

Portion: 1 slice of cake eaten with a cup of tea or coffee

Cakes, pies and pastries are delicious foods, and it would be foolish, and against the spirit of the **EATALL™** way, not to enjoy them. A piece of chocolate cake with chocolate icing is around 250 Calories for roughly four ounces. You can eat it, but do you really want to take in so many Calories for so very little bulk?

The main problem is the icing. Do without that and your slice of cake averages 100 Calories – an ideal **EATALL™** portion.

It would be tedious to consider the merits and demerits of each type of cake. It's enough to realize that a rich, buttery cake will probably run to 150 Calories for an average slice, an ordinary piece will run to around 100 Calories, and adding icing will shoot the Calorie count up to 250 or more.

Enjoy some cake every day if you love cake. Eat it slowly so that one portion lasts a long time. After a while you'll only want a small portion.

What about pies? Because commercially produced pies carry a lot of sugar, and slices of pie are generally larger than slices of cake, you have to think a slice of pie will run to around 250 to 300 Calories. Halve it, and you have something much more manageable.

Scones, Biscuits & Cookies

Portion: 1 or 2 mini-sized scones, biscuits or cookies

All these can be bought in mini sizes, perfect for an **EATALL™** portion. These small servings will run from 30 to 60 Calories, so enjoy one or two with a cup or tea or coffee, even if you drink these with milk.

Cookies make excellent **EATALL™** portions because it is so easy to eat from one to four, depending on their caloric value. They are also easy to carry around in the car, take on the plane, whatever.

Milk & Milk Drinks

Portion: ½ cup of full-fat milk or flavored milk, or 1 cup of reduced-fat milk.

A cup of full-fat milk carries 140 Calories, a cup of reduced fat milk around 100 Calories, and a cup of non-fat milk 80 Calories. The choices are clear. A small amount added to tea or coffee won't affect the Calorie count too much. Just use your best judgment.

Flavored milks will have added Calories because they carry added sugar as well as the flavoring. A cup of chocolate milk will have roughly 200 Calories.

Sodas & Fruit Juices

Portion: 1 tin diet soda with a cookie, or ½ cup fruit juice.

A cup of cranberry juice carries 140 Calories, orange juice around 120. If you dilute the juice with water you still get the flavor, the drink is much better at quenching thirst, and you don't overload your system with Calories or fruit in too intense a form.

Diet sodas have few Calories but contain a lot of salt. Just bear this in mind when drinking them. When in doubt, drink water.

Ice Cream

Portion: ½ cup of rich ice cream or a cup of light ice cream or frozen yogurt.

Ice cream varies between 140 Calories for half a cup of rich ice cream, to 100 Calories for half a cup of light ice cream. Frozen yogurt carries around 100 Calories for half a cup. A scoop is of ice cream - a small one, makes a good **EATALL™** portion.

Chocolate & Candy

Portion: 2 pieces of candy or chocolate

A piece of hard candy averages around 40 Calories, a piece of chocolate around 30 Calories for dark chocolate, 35 Calories for milk chocolate.

These portions make great desserts for an **EATALL™** meal.

A teaspoon of marmalade, jam or jelly carries around 40 Calories, a stick of gum 7. It's not hard to figure out an **EATALL™** portion. Remember to suck, not bite, and you'll enjoy more and eat less.

Snacks

Portion: 100 Calorie packs of any kind of snack

The supermarkets carry a fantastic variety of snacks and nibbles. Many packages are already presented in 100 Calorie packs, ideal for **EATALL™** portions. They're perfect packs to get you through the working day, for eating during meetings and for traveling.

Because these snacks are dry they don't cause problems while carrying or eating them. You can also combine them with vegetables – a tomato, a small carrot, a couple of radishes – and make a more substantial, healthy **EATALL™** portion.

Puddings

Portion: a single supermarket pack

The supermarkets display an enormous variety of puddings: jellies, custards and yogurts. You need to study the Calorie content as you shop. Generally a 4 oz (100g) portion can be as high as 150 Calories. You can find smaller portions, or fat free, sugar free versions.

Rice, Grains & Potatoes

Portion: 1 cup rice, 1 medium potato, 3 cups plain-popped corn

A cup of cooked rice varies between 100 and 150 Calories, and you can count roughly the same for grains of various types. Popcorn is useful because a big bag weighs a small amount, so an **EATALL™** portion looks enormous.

Potatoes are a delicious food, but a medium one will contain 100 Calories, and a yam perhaps 80 Calories.

All these are excellent foods; just eat the right portions.

EATALL™ Prescriptions

There isn't any food which is forbidden in the **EATALL™** way. The only requirement is that you eat throughout the day but that you keep to **EATALL™** portions. At first it will seem hard to know how much it's useful to eat at each **EATALL™** time, but the best part of this way of losing waist is that nothing is forbidden. If you eat more than you need to your body will eventually tell you. Just cut down on your portions gradually, then see if you're still hungry. If not, cut down until you're comfortable with your **EATALL™** portions.

OVERVIEW OF THE EATALL™ WAY

Keep fun things to eat everywhere you go. But, make sure that you aren't staring at food all the time. That way you have the snacks ready when you need them, but not so close that you're tempted to constantly eat between **EATALL™** times.

Whatever you like can be used. Keep small packages in a drawer, or a fridge or wherever you like. Eat them hot or cold or at room temperature. You choose. Just pick a few different types of foods you like to eat. Then try to choose some that are a little 'healthier' – you know what we mean.

If you're already on a diet, then keep on that diet if you like it and it seems to work. Adapt it to fit the **EATALL™** way. Easy food to nibble on are crackers, especially those with low sugar content. Crackers such as WheatThins™ and Triscuits™ varieties, pretzels (you can get them with chocolate coverings – avoid the high sugar coating with yogurt), chips, cookies, fruit, vegetables, chocolates, nuts, dry fruit, drinks, smoothies, popcorn, pizza slices, or small pieces of anything. Add to those cold cuts, cheese, meat, fish and the like and you can see that there is really no limit to what you can keep on eating. There is no need to avoid any particular food – unless you want to lose weight more quickly – and even then just limit the amount you eat at any time. Of course, the fewer total Calories you eat the more likely you are to lose weight quickly over any time period.

The aim is simply to eat enough so that you don't feel hungry and then to keep on eating throughout the day. Some people ask what happens if they eat a meal and don't feel hungry for hours afterward – read Thanksgiving, Christmas, Easter, Passover and so on. The brilliant answer is: keep on eating. You'll find you naturally want to eat less as you progress. Has your stomach shrunk or is that an old wives' tale? Whatever, the fact is that you simply don't need as much to keep happy. That, naturally, means that you're perhaps limiting Calorie intake. More importantly, you're ensuring that the food is eaten over a longer time period.

Tooth brushing

So, with all this eating, don't you need to brush your teeth all the time? Well, if you can and feel inclined to then go ahead. Remember too much brushing is also considered unwise – it can thin the enamel. Otherwise don't sweat it. You can easily use gums or mints that help keep those pesky bacteria at bay until you can do the normal cleaning. Or simply rinse your mouth with water.

Eating less sugar always helps as that is what those bugs love to use. Even so, a reasonable amount of cleaning is all you need. How many people really brush after each meal? Not many do in truth, yet they still get away with it. The **EATALL™** way isn't going to affect your teeth any more than standard meals or snacks do.

Clothing

Sorry about this. You'll have to have this adjusted, or go and buy some smaller stuff. When you start the method you may think your clothes just don't fit right, or that you have the wrong brand. Nope, that won't be it. You'll need to have them taken in. Worse things could happen. You may have to find a brand which caters for slimmer people. So many mass-produced clothes now have overweight shapes in mind, even in the smaller sizes. Women's pants are an example. As you lose fat and do some exercise your butt lifts. Find a brand which caters for this.

You can always give your old clothes to a charity. That can be a really uplifting experience, by the way. One time we got a letter saying how much an old suit helped another person get a badly needed job. So the method not only helps your figure, it can also help others in need.

Weighing Yourself

This is the hardest part of the method. We aren't sure that we should encourage this. Machines are usually inaccurate. The ones in the doctor's office seem to be consistent so rely on those. But otherwise the machines you can buy in hardware stores tend to be a gamble for accuracy. If you can keep one in the same place for a period of time then sure, go ahead and see what the relative weight loss is. Just don't change machines, and if yours seems to give random numbers then stop relying on it.

The best measure really is the waist measurement. You'll see your clothes cease to fit – that they feel more (or less, if you lose too much) comfortable. You may even find your feet shrink – you may need a half shoe size smaller, which means buying new shoes.

But if you insist on measuring your mass (that is weight at whatever altitude you happen to be at – I couldn't resist that, it's the scientist in me – sorry) then do so at a fixed time every day. The best time is in the morning after elimination. It's even better if you've just worked out and not had any liquids to drink. Whatever you decide to do, just be consistent or you won't have any useful information. Your weight can vary by two or three percent during the day. Some people fluctuate all the time within 3-4 lbs (1.5-2 kg) depending on their actual weight. The point is don't get disappointed at any particular time of day. If you drink lots of water, as is considered healthy, then that water will show as extra weight, and the machine will pick up on that.

THE FUTURE

We don't really know if a large proportion of the population will take on the **EATALL™** way of eating. But, if the number becomes large enough then we can hope that those who like to make a buck will start making **EATALL™** packs or portions. These can greatly aid the process for those of us who don't have the confidence or time to make them for ourselves. OK, maybe we're simply too lazy. We're willing to pay a price simply for the convenience.

These packs can be any type of food, and preferably a combination of such foods. They will be in amounts that the average person would eat every hour, or perhaps smaller so that you can choose to eat several different ones at a sitting. Maybe there will be packs for men, packs for women, packs for kids. There could be larger ones – double portions – so you can share with a friend.

Many of these packs already exist. Take a look at small packages in the supermarkets – even a bag of chips could count. The future will include more interesting items that will be easy to develop. They can be classified so that you can ensure that you get all the right vitamins, fiber, protein, even Calories – and whatever the latest fad food groups are – in your food.

You'll be able to simply eat one of every number every day and you'll achieve the right balance. That will definitely take the guesswork out of any food plan, and these little packages will be easy to carry around with you, or refrigerate and then microwave etc. There really is no limit to what can be done.

In the outside world – that is, in those wonderful places where kids love to eat, MickyD's and the like – maybe management will finally get the idea that even more money can be made by selling undersized, or mini sized portions – not super-sized ones. Making a profit was their main aim anyway, wasn't it? Surely they weren't really trying to make the Western world fat? The price set for each

EATALL™ portion will be less, but not that much less. And think how many more they can sell and people will go away happy.

People could be encouraged to drink more healthily, too. It's good to drink all the time, but it isn't a good idea to take in one's sugar that way. Of course the more fancy restaurants – OK, OK it does take a bit of a leap to be fancier, we're talking about those places where they use words like nouveau to describe their wares – already charge you more to eat less. The larger the plate, the smaller the portion seems to be their rule. They've got the right idea.

If you can afford to eat there, go for it, they're definitely on the right track. The problem is their sauces of course – usually packed full of sugar. Just be careful to eat the protein, the vegetables and leave the rice and other sugar laden components. But, in the future, those guys will make sure the portions are smaller still and are all great to eat.

Maybe we're just being naïve; then again, maybe not. The chance to make more money by selling less food, combined with having special new recipes that no one else has, can spur people into action.

Perhaps someone reading this will get the process going. Think of all the trademark potential, the franchises and the like. The bottom line is that the **EATALL™** way may be less natural to practice in the existing world – but it won't stay that way. That was also true for many diets, some of which were lifestyle changes also. Now you can buy packages of **Atkins™** food, **Weight Watchers™** meals and many others.

So, don't despair about losing weight. Try the **EATALL™** way, see how it works for you, find out whether you like it. Follow the suggestions, change them to suit you, turn the **EATALL™** way into your own, lifestyle way. It works – you can make it fit your lifestyle and work for you.

EATALL™ THE TRADEMARK

Richard practices intellectual property law. **EATALL™** is our trademark. Please treat it nicely. It can only be used as an adjective and not as a noun. But we all know that won't happen. Look what happened with Kleenex™ – people simply ask for a Kleenex not a Kleenex™ tissue, or for a Xerox, not a Xerox™ copy. It won't change and we really don't have the time to mess with you – but please try your best. That, by the way, is why when we use the word **EATALL™** in this book it's almost always followed by a noun and used with the ™ sign. Soon, we trust, to change into the R within a circle:®.

So please remember **EATALL™** is an adjective. It modifies a noun like 'portion' or 'way'. And Richard wonders why he has so few friends!

EPILOGUE

That's it, that's all there is to it. Snacking the **EATALL™** way to lose waist is easy, satisfying and effective. All you have to remember is:

> *Forget meals; instead, consume EATALL™ portions throughout your waking day, at frequent, approximately hourly, intervals.*

Remember, too, that you'll not only lose weight, as a further bonus you'll almost certainly extend your life as well as improve the quality of that life. Enjoy, good luck and a much-reduced waist!

ACKNOWLEDGMENTS

We would like to thank Sandra Aris, Kenneth Buechler, Tyler Callahan, Rachel Caputo, Anthony Christarella, Tony Elkin, Kathy Foster, Ruth James, Jeff Kauffman, Lisa Kieu, Diana Shaman, Nunthirat Suwannagate. Madeleine Warburg, Ruth Passow Warburg and many others, too numerous to mention, for their very generous help in the development of this book.

They all made valuable and helpful comments which helped us to improve the book; a number also took the trouble to try out the **EATALL™** methods. We know how much work it takes to keep accurate records, and very much appreciate the time these volunteers put into making sure that their experiences will help people trying the **EATALL™** way for the first time.

THE AUTHORS

Richard Warburg was born in England and attended University in Birmingham, England, earning both a B.S. (1978) and a Ph.D. (1981) in Biological sciences and Genetics, respectively. After spending several years as a postdoctoral research fellow at Brandeis University in Waltham, Massachussetts, including teaching a semester of biochemistry at Wellesley college, he started practicing as a patent agent in Boston, MA in 1985. When he graduated valedictorian from Suffolk University law school (1990) in Boston, he moved to California to practice intellectual property law in private practice.

Richard is recognized as an expert in intellectual property (IP) law and represents both small and large companies in all aspects. He has assisted clients in patent prosecution and litigation in various aspects of biology including technology used to sequence the human genome, to clone animals, and in the patenting of a healthy margarine that can lower blood cholesterol levels. He has also represented clients in other technologies including clothing, shoes and computer sciences. He lectures throughout the world, and is an author of several scientific and legal publications.

Richard invented a board game, the PATENTIAL® game, that is used as a tool to educate at school, university and industrial campuses in the biotechnology field, and in particular on development of pharmaceuticals. He is a coauthor of *Working to Improve Lives*, An Illustrated Biotech Encylopedia which uses the game to illustrate the biotech process.

Richard is an avid ballroom dancer and won the world amateur ballroom dance competition in Vegas, NV in 2007. He also paints using acrylics and the occassional oil on canvas. Some of his work can be found online at www.buypatential.com.

Tessa Lorant was born in Germany but moved to England with her family at an early age. She obtained a University of London BA in Mathematics, then moved to the United States for her first job. She worked as a computer programmer in New York City, then left to teach Pure Mathematics to undergraduates at the University of Wisconsin.

After completing her Masters Degree at Wisconsin she married an Englishman and returned to the UK. She has always had a keen interest in knitting, initiated by her university tutor, a geometer, who pointed out the connection between knitting and topology.

Tessa began writing on the topic of knitting and was immediately published by Batsford and Van Nostrand Reinhold. The books sold well, but the titles that were both immensely popular and important for the history of knitting were the ones she published as *The Heritage of Knitting Series,* brought out by The Thorn Press. She is now a respected and well-known writer on all aspects of hand and machine knitting, and already has a place in the seminal *A History of Hand Knitting,* by Richard Rutt. (Batsford 1987, Interweave Press 2003).

Tessa began to broaden her writing. She won the OddFellows Social Concern Award of 1987 with her book *A Voice At Twilight* (Peter Owen 1986). Other publications include three novels with HodderHeadline, under the name Emma Lorant.

Tessa continues to write both fiction and non-fiction. She is at present working on a family saga, a trilogy set in the US, Central Europe and the UK. The Thorn Press will publish the first volume, *The Dohlen Inheritance,* in February 2009.

Printed in the United States
145140LV00010B/159/P